Carola Schulz

The Identification of Critical Road Infrastructures – The Case of Baden-Wuerttemberg

The Identification of Critical Road Infrastructures – The Case of Baden-Wuerttemberg

by
Carola Schulz

KIT Scientific Publishing

Dissertation, Karlsruher Institut für Technologie
Fakultät für Wirtschaftswissenschaften
Tag der mündlichen Prüfung: 6.12.2011
Referenten: Prof. Dr. Werner Rothengatter, Prof. Dr. Ute Werner

Impressum

Karlsruher Institut für Technologie (KIT)
KIT Scientific Publishing
Straße am Forum 2
D-76131 Karlsruhe
www.ksp.kit.edu

KIT – Universität des Landes Baden-Württemberg und nationales
Forschungszentrum in der Helmholtz-Gemeinschaft

KIT Scientific Publishing 2012
Print on Demand

ISBN 978-3-86644-788-2

FOREWORD

Breakdowns in infrastructure networks reduce the functioning of logistics and the mobility of people and are detrimental to the market efficiency. Such disturbances can be caused by sudden and unforeseen events like natural catastrophes. In such cases it is very hard to find good solutions for managing the risk of failure, i.e. to combine precaution, mitigation and adaptation measures in an optimal way. A basic precondition for the design of best risk management strategies is the identification of the critical infrastructure elements, i.e. sections which are highly vulnerable and may cause large economic losses in case of crash.

In this book, Carola Schulz presents a new way to identify such critical infrastructures by combining network analysis, risk analysis and impact assessment. In general the indirect losses occurring through the interruption of economic activities are much higher than the direct damages, a fact which motivates her to focus on indirect losses, only. These losses can be measured by increased generalised costs occurring to the network users. As generalised costs consist of time losses and additional operation costs of the users it is evident that the assessment approach for indirect losses can be derived from transport modelling theory.

Carola follows the ideas of Nobel Prize Laureate D. McFadden who modelled the decisions of transport users as a hierarchy of discrete choices (trip making, choice of destination, transport mode and network route). The expected maximum utility (EMU) of the choices can be used as a welfare measure, which is quantified by means of a nested logit approach. Besides the theoretical consistency the advantage of this approach in the present context is that measurement and evaluation can be modelled in one step of calculation, because all "nests" of the decision hierarchy of the agents are integrated. Indirect economic losses then can be measured by a change of EMUs resulting from the increase of generalised costs caused by interruptions of transport flows.

This theoretical concept is applied within a large case study for the road transport network in Baden-Württemberg, assuming single and multiple simultaneous road closures. Furthermore, simulation studies for the impacts of an earthquake (according to an event in Ebingen that happened ca. 100 years ago) and of a flood (a fictional event in Esslingen) conclude the empirical investigations.

The reader will find in this book a clear concept for measuring and evaluating indirect economic losses and its application to identify critical road infrastructures. Furthermore, a rich and detailed case study demonstrates the practical value added by the model application and gives a better understanding of the order of magnitude of economic risks associated with critical road infrastructures.

Werner Rothengatter

ACKNOWLEDGMENTS

This dissertation would not have been possible without the support of many people and institutions. For lack of space, I am not able to mention everybody by name. Even though, my thanks are also directed to them.

I owe my gratitude to my supervisor, Prof. Dr. Werner Rothengatter, for his supporting guidance and the creative and pleasant working environment he established at the Institute. I would like to thank my co-referee Prof. Dr. Ute Werner for her invaluable encouragement, inspiration and advice during my studies and my thesis.

I am also very grateful to Prof. Dr. Friedemann Wenzel and Prof. Dr. Kay Mitusch for their valuable advice and the freedom they allowed me to have during my work.

This thesis would not have been possible without the professional, technical and psychological support of my colleagues, in particular Prof. Dr. Axel Schaffer, Dr. Gernot Liedtke, Dr. Aaron Scholz, Dr. (in spe) Lars Wessels and Dr. Mirjam Merz. They all, especially Axel, never stopped believing in the completion of my thesis and they were always full of good advice whenever I felt like throwing in the towel. I can't thank them enough.

I would also like to convey my thanks to my CEDIM colleagues Dr. Sergey Tyagunov and Dr. Andreas Kron for the provision of the scenarios and for patiently answering all my questions as well as to the PTV AG (Prof. Dr. Christoph Walther) for providing me with VALIDATE/VISUM and thereby enormously improving the quality of my calculations.

Special thanks also to the Ministerium für Umwelt, Naturschutz und Verkehr in Baden-Württemberg, the Innenministerium Baden-Württemberg as well as the Regierungspräsidium Tübingen, the Regierungspräsidium Freiburg, the Bundesministerium für Verkehr, Bau und Stadtentwicklung, the Deutscher Wetterdienst, the Forstliche Versuchs- und Forschungsanstalt Baden-Württemberg (Dr. Axel Albrecht, Dr. Ulrich Kohnle), CEDARthree Ltd. (Simon Langdon) and the Gesamtverband der Deutsche Versicherungswirtschaft e.V. (Dr. Olaf Burghoff, Stephan Thiebes) - they all were extraordinary helpful in the gathering of data and information.

Last but not least, I would like to thank my family and friends for their understanding and their loving support which substantially enabled me to write and complete this thesis.

Karlsruhe, December 2011 Carola Schulz

ABSTRACT

Modern societies highly depend on well-functioning infrastructures, especially in the Energy, Transport, Water and Telecommunication sectors. The protection of critical infrastructure (CI) against failures has widely been recognized in national and international activities, for example, in the European Directive 2008/114/EC "on the Identification and Designation of European Critical Infrastructure (ECI) and the Assessment of the Need to Improve their Protection". These activities mark elementary steps towards a greater awareness of possible societal risks associated with the disruption of CIs.

The superordinate goal of this thesis is to contribute to the current European, national and regional endeavours to identify critical hot spots in the road network that, in the event of a road infrastructure disruption, would entail great indirect losses to society. Indirect losses here refer to the degraded serviceability of a road section and the immediate negative economic impacts on road users associated with the disruption.

So far, in literature, the identification of hot spots in transportation networks has predominantly been based on dimensionless indices, and input-output models are used to evaluate the long-term economic effects associated with an infrastructure disruption. This thesis focuses on the short- and medium-term monetized economic effects generated by road users, which are affected by the closure of road sections. The size of the economic effects associated with each road section's disruption determines a ranking, which then serves as indicator for its criticality. Estimating the effects of a road infrastructure disruption on trip makers and their behaviour requires a transport model, which can be based on various types of submodels. A logit-based approach therein provides the option to even monetize changes in trip making decisions like destination or modal choice. This thesis builds on such a concept, and suggests a new monetized loss calculation methodology based on a single measure that captures changes on various trip making decision levels, and also accounts for the duration of disruption. Having so far concentrated on the disruption of single road sections, the thesis further introduces a systematization of the effects of simultaneous failures of multiple road sections. With this, it offers a reinterpretation of the criticality assessment depending on the combinations of affected links, and poses a novelty in this field of research.

The methodology is applied to the case study area of Baden-Wuerttemberg and its motorway network. Furthermore, the thesis combines the estimated indirect losses with a qualitative and a quantitative measure of susceptibility to failure. The results of this risk assessment reveal that the most critical links, based on the indirect loss ranking, are not necessarily the links with the highest level of risk.

Two road disrupting scenarios of an earthquake and a flood in Baden-Wuerttemberg demonstrate the applicability of the methodology in the context of multiple, simultaneous failures. The indirect losses turn out to be marginal compared to the physical damage associated with these events, depending on the seriousness of damage assumed. Even if indirect losses, in certain situations, may contribute to the overall losses only to a negligible extent, their assessment might still be valuable for reconstruction decisions.

Therefore, the thesis at hand contributes to answering important issues with regard to CI identification and the application of an indirect loss calculation methodology. It may assist practitioners and politicians in the design and implementation process of national or international CI activities.

Contents

List of Figures

List of Tables

Abbreviations

b	Business
c	Commuter
CI	Critical infrastructure
CIs	Critical infrastructures
CS	Consumer surplus
EMU	Expected Maximum Utility
EU	European Union
GDP	Gross domestic product
I-O	Input-Output
MTL	Medium-term losses
n-b	Non-business
OR	Occupancy rate
pc	Passenger car
RAV	Reduced average VOT
STL	Short-term losses
VOD	Value of distance
VOE	Value of externalities
VOT	Value of time
VTTS	Value of travel time savings

1 INTRODUCTION

1.1 MOTIVATION

In the past 30 years, the annual number of extreme weather- and climate-related events worldwide has tripled in comparison to the corresponding time span between 1950 and 1980 (Münchener Rückversicherungs-Gesellschaft (2011b)). These types of events account for about 70-80% of all economic losses caused by catastrophic events (European Environment Agency (2004), p.70; Münchener Rückversicherungs-Gesellschaft (2011a)). In the course of climate change they are projected to happen even more often. Therefore, economic losses due to weather- and climate-related events will increase if efforts in terms of prevention and disaster management are stagnating. Other recent non-weather-related incidents such as the enormous earthquake in Japan in 2011, with the triggered tsunami and the nuclear emergency, have demonstrated that, even in modern, presumably well-prepared societies, there are some vulnerabilities to natural and technological hazards with regard to which we are still far from being prepared.

Critical infrastructures (CIs) are especially sensitive to highly damaging events. The Deutsches Bundesamt für Sicherheit in der Informationstechnik (2004) defines CIs as "organizations and institutions that are important to public welfare; such that failure or disruption of them will result in long-lasting supply bottlenecks, significant disturbances in public security or have other dramatic consequences". CIs include, among others, energy supplies, telecommunications and information technology, as well as transportation systems. Due to their societal importance, it is crucial to understand how their functionality might be impacted on by disruptions.

The European Commission acknowledged this need in Directive 2008/114/EC "on the identification and designation of European Critical Infrastructure and the assessment of the need to improve their protection". European critical infrastructures (ECI) are CIs located in the EU, whose disruption would significantly affect at least two Member States. The significance of the impact is measured using three criteria: casualties, economic effects and public effects.

The focus, here, is on the economic effects. After a disaster, headlines in newspapers often publish the amount of economic losses. These losses usually only refer to direct damages. This means that only physical damage to houses and infrastructure in terms of reconstruction costs or insured losses are taken into account. However, the notion of economic losses makes one assume that other costs such as business interruption costs, detouring costs, environmental costs, etc. should be included. These losses belong to the category of indirect costs, which constitute the largest cost component in transportation and communication sector failures (ECLAC (2003)). While, nowadays, direct costs can be projected relatively easy before an event (scenario-based) or estimated with the help of remote sensing or insurance data after an event, the determination of indirect costs still poses an enormous challenge.

This thesis focuses on the estimation of indirect costs imposed by disrupted transportation networks. Transportation networks are embedded in the socio-economic functions of individuals, organizations and institutions, as they are crucial for the continuity of many business activities and for the basic supply of food and other essential goods. As a result, there is a great societal interest in having reliable networks. If transport is disrupted or ceases to operate, the consequences can be dramatic. Road networks are especially interesting in this respect, because car drivers make their decisions individually, with no central optimising institution (such as exists with regard to rail networks). The comprehensive network, the possibility of it being used by various types of vehicles, as well as flexible travel scheduling, makes it attractive and essential for both freight and passenger transportation. Thus, for example, in 2008, ca. 87% of passenger transport performance and ca. 71% of freight transport performance were carried out on the road network (Deutsches Institut für Wirtschaftsforschung (2010)).

The superordinate goal of this thesis is to contribute to the current European, national and regional endeavours to identify hot spots in the road network that, in case of a disruption, would entail great indirect losses, in other words, whose indirect loss potential is very high.

The target groups at which this work is aimed are, on the one hand, the research community and, on the other, policy makers and authorities engaged in critical infrastructure protection as well as in disaster control and management.

1.2 Structure

This study unfolds as follows. First Chapter 2 introduces the concept of CIs in the context of national and international activities and explains relevant notions related to CIs. Studies on historical road disruption events contribute to the predication, in terms of how road users are affected by limitations in the serviceability of a road infrastructure. The chapter then gives an overview of the indirect loss calculation methodologies and CI identification approaches currently present in the field to identify research gaps.

Chapter 3 first substantiates the objectives of this study based on the findings of the literature review. Then it presents the calculation methodology with its relevant formulas to estimate the indirect losses which further serve as a criticality measure for the identification of critical road infrastructures. This is followed by an approach to interpret the interdependencies of different road sections and infrastructures in the context of CI identification.

Thereafter, in Chapter 4, the case study area of Baden-Wuerttemberg with its road network is presented, followed by a compilation of assumptions, modeling requirements and available data. After giving a detailed description of the modeling procedure, relevant measures for analyzing the results are introduced.

Chapter 5 presents the results of the application of the loss calculation methodology and the corresponding CI identification to the Baden-Wuerttemberg case study. The findings are also compared with other potential indicators of criticality and are discussed against the background of bonus/malus payments with regard to construction sites. Finally the chapter sets the results in the context of a risk analysis.

In Chapter 6, two realistic scenarios of natural events, an earthquake and a flood, demonstrate simultaneous failures of multiple roads, interdependent effects and the application of the loss calculation technique to specific events. The calculated indirect losses are contrasted with the estimated physical damages in the scenarios.

Chapter 7 finally summarizes the most important findings of this study and points out potential areas for further research.

2 DEFINITIONS AND LITERATURE REVIEW

This chapter aims to set this study in the context of the respective field of research and defines and explains the relevant terms and concepts. First the concept of CIs is introduced against a background of national and international political agendas. The notion of risk and its components are closely connected to CIs and are hence introduced, focusing on the topic of this study: the road infrastructure. When analyzing activities on road infrastructure it is the trip making behavior and the decisions of the trip-makers that requires further attention. The subsequent chapters therefore present the basics of trip making behavior using the classic four steps of transport modeling, and explicate how the different steps are affected by road closures. This is done by analyzing empirical studies on historical road disruption events. Finally this chapter gives an overview and contrasts existing indirect loss calculation methodologies and CI identification approaches present in current research. The identified research deficits then serve as basis for the objectives and the proceedings of this study.

2.1 CRITICAL INFRASTRUCTURES (CIS)

The term 'critical infrastructure' (CI) has evolved parallel to the world-wide distribution of the internet and the broad interconnection that has come with it. In this context, it has been realized that a small disturbance at a critical node could have major effects on the rest of the network. Clearly, this problem is not limited to cyber networks but can also be observed with regard to the increasingly interconnected power supply system or transportation networks. In November 2006, for example, a controlled shutdown of a power line in Germany caused cascading failures not only in Germany, but also in France, Italy, Spain, Portugal, Croatia, Belgium and the Netherlands. As a consequence, 15 million European households experienced a temporary power supply disruption (UCTE (2007), p.11). CIs generally refers to society's lifelines, whose loss of serviceability may entail significant negative social and economic effects (Lenz (2009), p.13). In contrast to the concept of risk, which also takes into account causal events and their likelihood of occurrence, the term CI mainly emphasizes the potential consequences of a disrupting event.

With an increasing number of natural catastrophes, the continuing threat of terrorism, and complex technical interdependencies between lifelines, the protection of CIs has become one of the major concerns of national Civil Defence. However, the consequences of terrorist attacks or natural disasters hardly ever stop at national borders as can be seen in the examples mentioned above. Therefore, various initiatives have already been taken, particularly in the field of cyber security, to provide a better response to these kinds of incidents on an international level[1]. Besides, miscellaneous national and international activities to identify and protect CIs were set on political agendas. The following two chapters summarize the political actions on the European and German level. Subsequently, the issue of interdependencies between CI sectors as one aspect of CIs is discussed.

2.1.1 European actions concerning CIs

In June 2004, three months after the bombings in Madrid, the European Council asked the European Commission for the preparation of an overall strategy for CI protection. The Commission responded in October 2004 with a communication on "Critical Infrastructure Protection in the Fight Against Terrorism", which suggested enhancements of the European prevention of and response to terrorist attacks in respect of CIs. The CIs involved covered all sectors. In November 2005, the Commission, upon request of the European Ministers in December 2004, adopted a Green Paper on a "European Programme for Critical Infrastructure Protection (EPCIP)". The Green Paper raises questions and ideas as to how an EPCIP could be set up, and leaves these issues for discussions with stakeholders (Fritzon et al. (2007)). The suggested goal of the EPCIP is "to ensure that there are adequate and equal levels of protective security on critical infrastructure, minimal single points of failure and rapid, tested recovery arrangements throughout the Union" (Commission of the European Communities (2005)). A draft Directive (Commission of the European Communities (2006b)) and another communication (Commission of the European Communities (2006a)) were published in December 2006 and finally resulted in a modified version which was adopted as Directive 2008/114/EC "on the Identification and Designation of European Critical Infrastructure (ECI) and the Assessment of the Need to Improve their Protection".

The goal of the Directive is to "establish a procedure for the identification and designation of European Critical Infrastructures (ECIs'), and a common approach to the assessment of the need to improve the protection of such infrastructures in order to contribute to the protection of the people" (Council of the European Union (2008)). The Directive defines CI as "an asset, system or part thereof located in Member States which is essential for the maintenance of vital societal functions, health, safety, security, economic or social well-being of people, and the

[1] Existing international initiatives mainly concern computer/information technology, e.g. Forum of Incident Response and Security Teams (FIRST) and European Network and Information Security Agency (ENISA).

disruption or destruction of which would have a significant impact in a Member State as a result of the failure to maintain those functions". Due to the European character of the CI, the Directive also defines the European Critical Infrastructure (ECI) as a "critical infrastructure located in Member States the disruption or destruction of which would have a significant impact on at least two Member States. The significance of the impact shall be assessed in terms of cross-cutting criteria. This includes effects resulting from cross-sector dependencies on other types of infrastructure". The mentioned cross-cutting criteria comprise casualties, economic effects (including the impact on the environment) and public effects (e.g. public confidence). The precise thresholds for when the potential impact in regard to the criteria is big enough to comply with the ECI definition is left to the member states to decide, and shall be done on a case-by-case basis. The Directive follows an all hazard approach, taking into account every possible cause of disruption, including terrorism. It includes solely the energy and transport sectors, with the option for a later amendment to include other sectors, especially the information and communication technology (ICT) sector. The reporting duties on part of the member states do not include the location or potential impact of the identified ECI. The responsibility for securing and protecting CIs still lies with the specific operators or member states.

The Directive in its current form cannot fulfil the ambitious goals originally intended in the first communication and paper in 2004. Its practical purpose is more to foster bi- or trinational discussions between member states on CIs that might have cross border effects (which were partly already in place before the Directive), and to start a maturing process in ECI protection. The Directive had to be implemented by 12th January, 2011. Many of the countries follow the non-binding guidelines issued confidentially by the Council in November 2008 for the application of the cross-cutting criteria and thresholds that could be used in the identification process. There are still many issues open in the implementation process concerning the thresholds, methodologies and responsibilities within the member states (e.g. the Ministry of Civil Protection is in charge of the implementation but the know-how is in other Ministries such as Energy/Transport). These issues and the still maturing process of the Directive leave many questions open to research on CIs and their identification and protection.

2.1.2 *German actions concerning CIs*

Beside the international initiative of the European Union, there are also activities at national levels. Similar to the European Directive, the German national initiative on the protection of CIs under the Federal Ministry of the Interior defines CIs as "organizational and physical structures and facilities of such vital importance to a nation's society and economy that their failure or degradation would result in sustained supply shortages, significant disruption of public safety and security, or other dramatic consequences" (BMI (2009a), p.4).[2] After the terrorist attacks in New York 2001 and Madrid 2004 the German Federal Office of Civil Protection and Disaster Assistance (BBK) (founded in 2004) identified CI protection as one of their major tasks. CIs can usually be found in the following infrastructural sectors (BMI (2007), p.10):

- Information and Telecommunication Technology
- Energy
- Traffic and Transport
- Supply (food supply, water supply, waste water disposal, emergency/ rescue services, healthcare)
- Monetary System, Finance and Insurance
- Authorities and Public Administration
- Hazardous Materials
- Other CIs (media, cultural property, major research facilities)

Figure 1 presents a general (left pyramid in the background) and a specific systematic overview (right pyramid) of the classification of CIs. The right pyramid highlights the transport and traffic sector, which is the topic of this study.

[2] An overview of how other countries define CIs can be found in Lenz (2009), p.18.

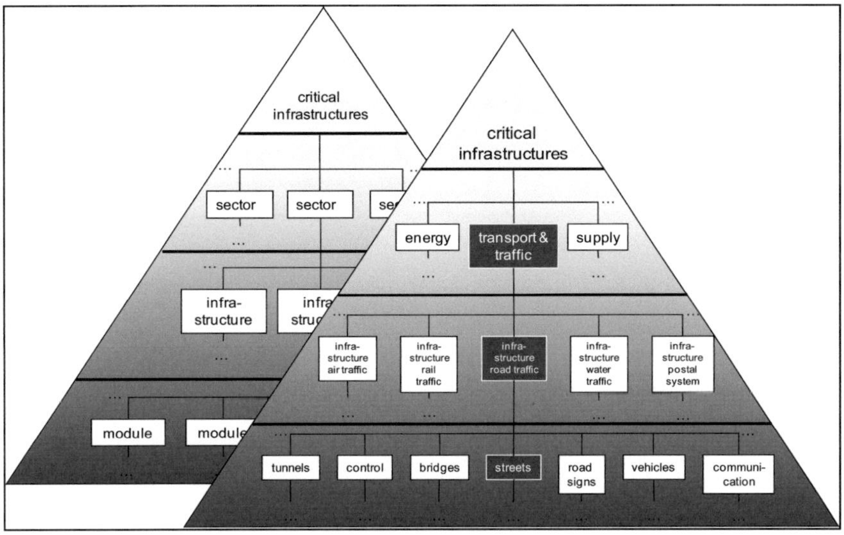

Figure 1: Systematization of CIs (own illustration based on Lenz (2009), p.22f)

The CI sectors and the definition of CIs are essentially the same in other national activities. Commonly, countries define CIs according to their potential impact in the event of disruption. While there might actually be no differences in the practical application of the definitions, the wording of the definitions display slight differences in the understanding of cross-border responsibilities in respect of CIs. For instance, Canada's definition of CIs explicitly relates to the impact on the citizens or the government of Canada (Public Saftey Canada (2009)), unlike, for example, Switzerland's definition (Schweizerische Eidgenossenschaft (2009)), which does not further specify the addressees of the impacts.

2.1.3 Interdependencies between CIs

In accordance with the definitions of CIs as given above, it is not the infrastructures themselves, but rather the services they provide, that are crucial and valuable to society (e.g. Little (2002)). The provision of services often intertwines between different infrastructural sectors as depicted in Figure 2.

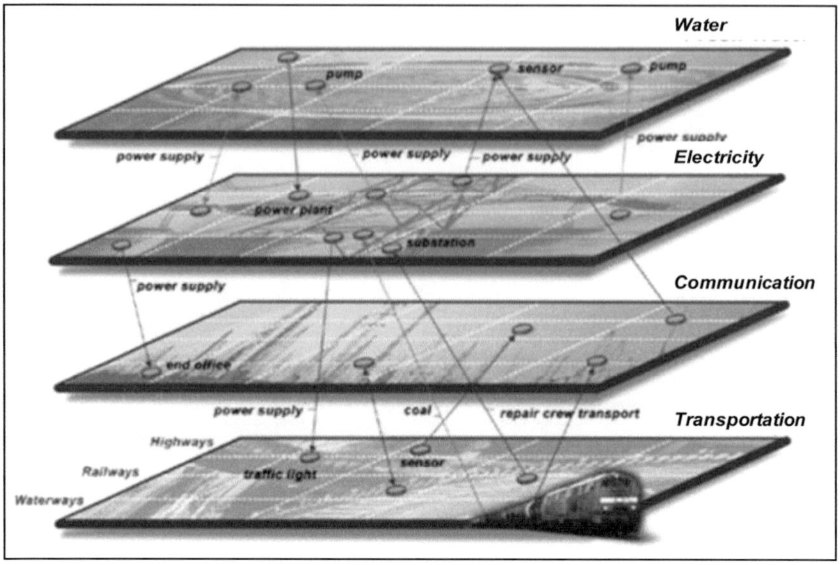

Figure 2: Complex interaction of infrastructure (Karlsruhe Cluster for Disaster Research (2006), p.14)

Rinaldi et al. (2001) structure (inter)dependencies between infrastructures based on the nature of the linkage: physical, cyber, geographical or logical. A physical interdependency, for example, exists between a coal-fired power station and railways delivering coal, which simultaneously need the energy generated from the power station for their locomotion. An example of cyber interdependencies poses the linkage between information-based power generation and the necessity of power for the information generation. Spatial proximity fosters geographical interdependencies in case of an event, like a flood, when multiple infrastructure elements are affected simultaneously. If an interdependency mechanism is not of a geographical, cyber or physical nature, it falls into the category of logical interdependencies, often characterized by the involvement of human decisions. An example of the latter is a local power outage and the subsequent need for people to communicate more with each other, leading to a capacity overload of the communications network.

Research in this area takes the criticality of the sectors as given. The main interest is therefore not the identification of CI elements in the CI sectors, but to identify interdependencies between sectors, and to model their interdependent mechanisms to capture, for example, the cascading effects of interrupting events. The methodologies for modeling the interdependencies between CIs or cascading effects originating in one CI range from system dynamics (e.g. Dauelsberg and Outkin (2005); Bush et al. (2005)), Spatial Computable General Equilibrium (SCGE) (e.g. Zhang and Peeta (2011)), agent-based modeling (e.g. Cardellini et al. (2007)), social network analysis (e.g. Zhang et al. (2008)), network theory (e.g. Peters et al. (2008)) to input-output interoperability modeling using the Leontief influence matrix (e.g. Haimes and Jiang (2001); Setola et al. (2009); Reed et al. (2007)). Pederson et al. (2006) give an overview of the research efforts occupied with the modeling of CI interdependencies.

The Swiss Federal Office for Civil Protection suggests an expert survey-based analysis of the interdependencies between CI sectors in order to assess the criticality of infrastructure subsectors according to their dependencies (BABS (2010)). The exemplary qualitative dependency assessment depicted in Table 1 gives an overview of the severity of the consequences of a three week subsector total failure in Switzerland imposed on other subsectors. Disruptions in road transportation, for example, entail huge effects on the 'public safety, rescue and emergency services' sector, which also highly depends on the sectors 'Information and communication technology' as well as on 'Energy'.

This type of qualitative interdependency analysis is suggested as part of the identification of CIs in Switzerland. Without doubt, dependencies between subsectors contribute to the dimensions of criticality, but in order to identify concrete CI elements, an analysis of the exact serviceability disruptions, interdependencies and their mechanisms is inevitable.

Critical Infrastructure Protection Working Group (CIP WG), coregroup criticality

Dependencies between subsectors
(direct effects of a subsector's total failure in whole Switzerland for a duration of 3 weeks)

Degree:
0 = no
1 = little
2 = big
3 = huge

Sector	Subsector	No.	Public administration				Chemical industrie	Energy			Waste disposal			Financial services		Public health			Information and communication technology (ICT)					Water and food		Public safety, rescue and emergency services			Transportation					**Total** (dependencies caused by subsector)	Number of affected subsectors (>0)	Average Dependency
		Subsector	Parliament, government, justice, administration	Research institutes	National cultural property	Foreign repres./ headquarters of int. Org.	Production, transp., storage and proc. of chem.	Power supply	Oil supply	Natural gas supply	Wastewater	Industrial and domestic waste	Special waste	Banks	Insurance companies	Medical care and hospitals	Medication	Laboratories	Telecommunication	Information systems and networks	Internet	Instrumentation, autom. and monit. systems	Radio and media	Food supply and food security	Drinking water supply	Emergency organisations	Protection & Support service	Army	Road transport	Rail transport	Air transport	Navigation	Postal services and logistics			
Sector	Subsector	No.	101	102	103	104	105	106	107	108	109	110	111	112	113	114	115	116	117	118	119	120	121	122	123	124	125	126	127	128	129	130	131			
Public administration	Parliament, government, justice, administration	1		0	0	1	0	0	0	0	0	0	0	1	1	0	0	0	0	0	0	0	1	0	0	1	1	3	0	0	0	0	0	9	7	1
	Research institutes	2	0		0	0	0	0	0	0	0	0	0	0	0	0	0	0	0	0	0	0	0	0	0	0	0	0	0	0	0	0	0	0	0	0
	National cultural property	3	1	0		0	0	0	0	0	0	0	0	0	0	0	0	0	0	0	0	0	0	0	0	0	0	0	0	0	0	0	0	1	1	1
	Foreign representations/ headquarters of international organisations	4	1	0	0		0	0	0	0	0	0	0	0	0	0	0	0	0	0	0	0	0	0	0	0	0	0	0	0	0	0	0	1	1	1
Chemical industrie	Production, transport, storage and processing of chemicals	5	0	1							1						2	2							1									7	5	1
Energy	Power supply	6	2	2	1	2	3		2	1	3	2	2	3	2	3	2	3	3	3	3	3	3	2	3	2	2	2	1	3	2	1	2	68	30	2
	Oil supply	7		1	0	0	2	0		0	0	0	0	0	0	0	0	1	0	0	0	0	0	2	0	2	2	2	3	1	3	3	2	24	12	2
	Natural gas supply	8	0	0	0	0	1	0	0		0	0	0	0	0	0	0	0	0	0	0	0	0	0	0	0	0	0	1	0	0	0	1	3	3	1
Waste disposal	Wastewater	9	1	1	1	1	1	0	0	0		1	1	1	1	2	0	1	1	0	0	0	1	0	1	1	1	1	0	1	1	0	0	20	19	1
	Industrial and domestic waste	10	1	1	0	1	1	0	0	0	0		1	1	1	2	0	1	1	0	0	0	1	0	1	1	1	1	1	0	0	0	0	17	16	1
	Special waste	11	0	1	0	0	1	0	0	0	0	0		0	0	1	0	1	0	0	0	0	0	0	0	0	0	0	0	0	0	0	0	4	4	1
Financial services	Banks	12	1	1	0	1	1	2	2	1	0	0	0		3	1	0	0	2	1	1	0	1	3	0	1	0	1	0	1	1	1	2	28	20	1
	Insurance companies	13	1	1	0	0	0	0	0	0	0	0	0	3		1	0	0	0	0	0	0	0	0	0	0	0	0	0	0	0	0	0	6	4	1
Public health	Medical care and hospitals	14	0	0	0	0	0	0	0	0	0	0	0	0	0		0	2	0	0	0	0	0	0	0	1	0	0	0	0	0	0	0	3	2	1
	Medication	15	0	0	0	0	0	0	0	0	0	0	0	0	0	3		1	0	0	0	0	0	0	0	2	0	0	0	0	0	0	0	6	3	2
	Laboratories	16	0	0	0	0	0	0	0	0	0	0	0	0	0	2	1		0	0	0	0	0	0	0	0	0	0	0	0	0	0	0	3	2	1
Information and communication technology (ICT)	Telecommunication	17	2	1	0	1	1	2	1	1	0	1	1	3	2	2	0	1		2	3	3	2	0	0	3	3	3	1	1	2	1	2	45	25	2
	Information systems and networks	18	2	2	1	1	1	1	0	0	1	0	1	3	2	2	1	1	3		3	3	2	1	1	2	1	2	1	2	2	1	2	45	27	2
	Internet	19	2	1	0	1	0	0	0	0	0	0	0	2	1	1	0	0	2	2		2	2	1	0	1	0	1	0	1	1	0	1	22	16	1
	Instrumentation, automation and monitoring systems	20	1	1	0	1	1	2	1	0	1	0	1	1	0	1	0	1	2	2	0		0	1	1	1	0	1	1	2	2	1	0	26	21	1
	Radio and media	21	2	1	0	0	0	0	0	0	0	0	0	1	0	1	0	0	1	0	0	2		0	1	2	0	1	1	1	0	0	0	14	11	1
Water and food	Food supply and food security	22	0	0	0	0	0	0	0	0	0	0	0	0	0	0	0	0	0	0	0	0	0		0	0	0	0	0	0	0	0	0	0	0	0
	Drinking water supply	23	0	1	0	0	0	1	0	0	1	0	0	0	0	2	0	1	0	0	0	0	0	0		1	0	1	0	0	0	0	0	8	7	1
Public safety, rescue and emergency services	Emergency organisations	24	1	0	1	0	0	0	0	0	0	0	0	0	0	1	0	0	0	0	0	0	0	0	0		2	1	1	0	1	0	0	8	7	1
	Protection & Support service	25	0	0	0	0	0	0	0	0	0	0	0	0	0	0	0	0	0	0	0	0	0	0	0	1		1	0	0	0	0	0	2	2	1
	Army	26	0	0	0	1	0	0	0	0	0	0	0	0	0	0	0	0	0	0	0	0	0	0	0	1	1		0	0	0	0	0	3	3	1
Transportation	Road transport	27	1	1	1	1	1	1	2	1	1	3	2	0	0	1	2	1	1	1	0	1	2	2	1	3	3	3		1	1	1	3	42	27	1
	Rail transport	28	1	0	0	0	2	0	2	0	0	1	2	0	0	0	1	0	0	0	0	0	1	2	0	0	0	2	0		1	2	2	19	12	1
	Air transport	29	0	1	0	2	1	0	0	0	0	0	0	0	0	0	1	0	0	0	0	0	1	1	0	0	0	0	0	0		0	1	8	7	1
	Navigation	30	0	0	0	0	2	0	2	0	0	0	0	0	0	0	0	0	0	0	0	0	0	1	0	0	0	0	0	0	0		0	5	3	2
	Postal services and logistics	31	1	1	0	1	1	0	0	0	0	0	0	1	1	1	1	1	1	0	0	0	1	1	0	0	0	1	0	0	0	0		13	13	1

Table 1: Exemplary assessment of dependencies between different sectors (own illustration based on the German version in BABS (2010), p.10)

Thus the identification of CIs usually starts with a single sector analysis and interdependencies are, if at all, taken into account at a later stage. This study concentrates on the road transportation network as one of the CI sectors. Interdependencies are not the focus of this work.

2.2 CI IN THE CONTEXT OF RISK

The concept of CI blends to a great extent into the term 'risk'. Since a lot of research efforts have already been spent on the different aspects of risk, the established methodologies and findings may be transferred into CI research. The definition of risk varies slightly between disciplines and between authors[3]. In the context of CIs, the following definition (e.g. Beer and Ziolkowski (1995), p.22; PCC RARM (1997), p.1) seems most appropriate:

$$\text{Risk} = \text{hazard} \times \text{consequences} \tag{2-1}$$

Risk is the product of the probability of an event (hazard) in a specific time span, and the expected consequences of such an event. While some research areas also associate risk with positive chances, here risk has only a negative connotation. Thus, it may also be explained as the expected negative consequences or expected losses within a time period.

In contrast to the concept of risk, the definition of CI primarily emphasizes the consequences of any possible disrupting event. The analysis of potential consequences has therefore priority, and the assessment of the probability of a disturbing incident (hazard) is of minor importance. Regardless of the likelihood of the disruption, if the potential consequences exceed a threshold with "dramatic" or "significant" impacts (BMI (2009a), p.4), the associated infrastructure is considered to be critical. Figure 3 illustrates this context.

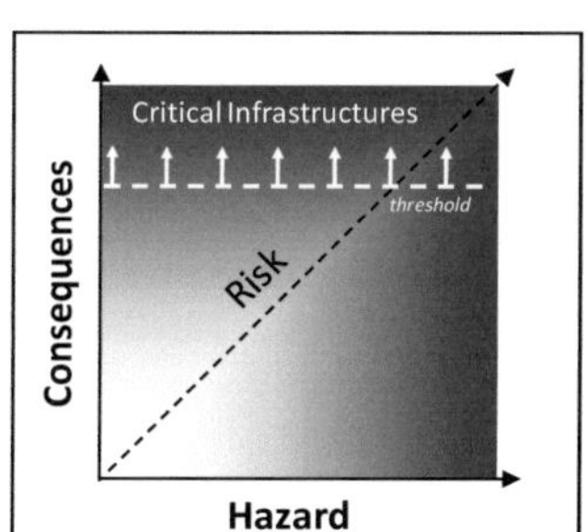

Figure 3: CIs in the context of risk

[3] An overview of definitions in the context of risk and risk analysis taking into account EU legislation can be found in European Commission (2010).

In the definition of risk, ‘consequences’ are interchangeable with ‘vulnerability’ to a hazard (see, for example, Garatwa and Bollin (2002); Markau (2003), p.24) or ‘vulnerability’ multiplied with the ‘exposure’ to a hazard (e.g. Thywissen (2006); Birkmann (2007)). The following example illustrates the difference between risk, vulnerability and exposure.

Assume there is the hazard of flooding in a region. The flood with a water level of 5m above normal and an approximate duration of three days happens with a probability of 1% per annum. This is the ‘hazard’. Affected by such an incident would be the ground floor of one company containing 2 machines (worth 50,000 Euro each) and the basement (with all its contents) of one house (worth 2,000 Euro). This is the ‘exposure’ to the hazard. ‘Vulnerability‘ expresses the expected consequences to the exposed elements (dependent on their susceptibility characteristics) in respect to the specific hazard. Here it is assumed that 100% of the machines and 50% of the basement content will be destroyed. The cleaning up would cost 1,000 Euro in total. The production downtime in the company would cost 10,000 Euro. The risk would then be 1% × (100% × 50,000 × 2 + 50% × 2,000+ 1,000 + 10,000) Euro=1,120 Euro per annum. The integral of the risk of all possible flooding events would be the risk of flooding in this region. The company in this example could reduce the risk, for example, by physical measures (e.g. setting up the machines on higher ground or making them flood proof) or operational measures (e.g. implementing a warning system).

Usually, vulnerability considers the susceptibility to events with everything that attenuates or amplifies the effects. But some authors also explicitly account for the resilience or coping capacity of the actors and assets in the risk formula (e.g. Lenz (2009)). Eventually, the subject-matter of a study determines the required level of detail in the formula. The simple formula (2-1) including hazard and consequences best describes the terms relevant to this study.

In order to identify CIs, the potential negative consequences of a disrupting event, from now on also called its ‘loss potential’, are of main concern. In this context, the European Directive 2008/114/EC or other CI programs ask for an all hazard approach. This means that every imaginable natural, technological or man-made hazard should be taken into account as a possible cause of an interruption and its impact. The events’ likelihood is, however, negligible for the designation of CIs. Yet, for the identification and justification of appropriate CI protection measures, the expected losses (the risk) need to be evaluated. The fact that a specific incident with its significant impacts can happen may already give enough reason to seriously consider countermeasures. An available estimation of the expected economic losses is nonetheless very helpful in cost-benefit assessments of countermeasures and the justification for public spending.

The following chapter takes a closer look at the possible unexpected[4] incidents causing a disruption of a road section[5]. Considering the case study area in the later chapters, the hazard analysis specifically focuses on the situation in Germany and in Baden-Wuerttemberg in particular. Section 2.2.2 then provides a more differentiated understanding of the potential consequences.

2.2.1 Hazards affecting road infrastructure

The Ministry of the Interior of Germany indicates a list of hazards and their possible impact on roads and other CI sectors (BMI (2007); BMI (2009b)). There are three categories: natural hazards, technological hazards/human failures and terrorist attacks/crime/war (see Table 2). In some cases the categories' distinction may not be very clear as the following example demonstrate.

Natural events	Technical failure/ human error	Terrorism, crime, war
Extreme weather events inter alia, storms, heavy precipitation, drops of temperature, floods, heat waves, droughts	System failure inter alia, insufficient or excessive complexity of planning, defective hardware and/or software bugs	Terrorism
Forest and heathland fires	Negligence	Sabotage
Seismic events	Accidents and emergencies	Other forms of crime
Epidemics and pandemics in man, animals and plants	Failures in organization inter alia, shortcomings in risk and crisis management, inadequate coordination and co-operation	Civil wars and wars
Cosmic events Inter alia, energy storms, meteorites and comets		

Table 2: Hazards affecting CIs (BMI (2009b), p.9)

Natural Events

In the past, weather-related events like fog, storms, extreme temperatures and floods have quite often affected roads' serviceability in Germany. Among the weather-related events, winter storms are especially worth mentioning. Storms harm the serviceability of the road infrastructure mainly through uprooted trees or other road-blocking materials. Baden-Wuerttemberg's expected maximum wind speeds exceed 24.5 m/s (measured 10 meters above

[4] Expected disrupting events are, for example, conventional construction works.

[5] An overview of hazards in respect to rail infrastructure can be found in Ott (2006) (in German) as well as in Ott and Schulz (2007) (in English).

the ground with a mean return period of 50 years) basically everywhere (see Figure 4). This corresponds to a wind force of 10 Bft (Beaufort scale), and is strong enough to uproot trees. At wind speeds above 17.2 m/s (wind force 8 Bft) branches may be blown down (SWR1 Aktuelle Information (2007)). The exact likelihood of a tree being uprooted or a branch falling at a specific wind speed is impossible to determine. Apart from the characteristics of the tree in respect of deep or shallow root building, age, height, width and health which may influence the likelihood of uprooting, the location relative to other trees also matters. There is, however, no clear relationship between the relative location of a tree and its likelihood of being uprooted. A tree within a group of trees is better protected against the wind by the surrounding trees, but its roots may not be as widely and deeply spread in the ground than the ones from trees with hardly any surrounding trees. It is therefore not possible to calculate the likelihood of a specific tree or group of trees blocking a road (Kohnle, U., Forstliche Versuchs- und Forschungsanstalt Baden-Württemberg, personal communication, 16.9.2009). Obviously, only trees in the vicinity of roads pose a threat. The easiest way to prevent disruption is therefore to remove all trees close enough to affect a road in the event of a storm. After the heavy storm entitled 'Lothar' in 1999, many trees have been cut along roads in the Baden-Wuerttemberg area. Lothar arrived on 26th December 1999 and devastated vast areas in Baden-Wuerttemberg, especially in the Black Forest. Many main, state and district roads, as well as railway tracks within the Black Forest were closed due to blocking by uprooted trees and branches. The A8 motorway near Pforzheim and parts of the A5 near Freiburg were also disrupted by trees (SWR1 Aktuell (1999); SWR Politik und Gesellschaft (1999)).

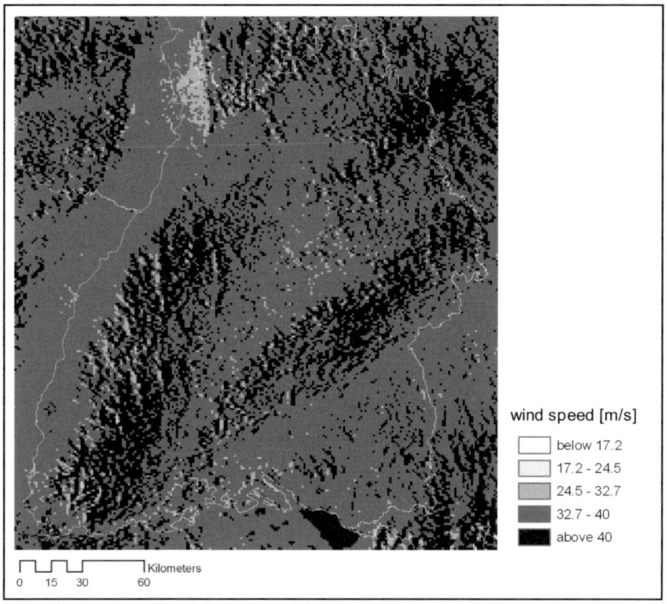

Figure 4: Maximum gust speeds in Baden-Wuerttemberg with an exceedance probability of 0.02 per year (equals a mean return period of 50 years) (original data based on Heneka et al. (2006))

Apart from winter storms, extreme weather events or climatic settings have the potential to seriously demolish the road infrastructure, so that the probability of accidents rises significantly. For example, in the winter of 2010, extraordinarily cold temperatures demolished the asphalt road surfaces of many regional roads. The direct damage to state roads amounted to approximately 5-10 million Euro (UVM (2010)). The duration of the low temperature period, together with the large amount of snow, entailed a shortage in the salt supply for road servicing. Consequently, iced road surfaces and snow added to the accident risk already caused by the frost damage. In the summer of the same year, the A8 motorway near Kirchheim u. T. had to be closed because high temperatures caused a buckling of the concrete road surface (Goll (2010)).

Another prominent weather-related cause of road disruptions are floods. The major rivers passing Baden-Wuerttemberg are the Danube, the Rhine and the Neckar. It happens now and then that even some major roads get flooded, as in August 2007, when a small section of the A5 motorway close to Efringen-Kirchen was overflown by the Rhine river (Spiegel Online GmbH (2007)). Thanks to flood protection measures such as dikes, major losses due to flooding have not occurred in the state in recent years. However, dikes may fail in extreme flooding situations, and therefore this type of hazard is still present. The seriousness of the physical damage to road infrastructure due to a flood depends significantly on the water level and the velocity of the water (Kunert (2010), p.245). Kunert (2010) suggests 6 damage levels as explained in more detail in Table 3.

damage scale	characteristics of damage to road
0	wet, dirty
1	maceration of soil, entailing damage of pavement superstructure
2	slight damage or slump, partly with water infiltrated into road surface
3	superficial damage, partly slumped and underwashed
4	serious damage to road and pedestrian pavement (cracks)
5	Very strong plane damage (including water disposal) as well as underwashing of base-layer and surface, partly broken off elements

Table 3: Scale of physical damages to road infrastructures caused by floods (based on Kunert (2010), p.241)

The seriousness of the physical damage and the duration of the water overflow highly influence the extent of the indirect losses. The last major flood in Germany happened in 2002 in Saxony. On 12th to 13th August 2002 heavy rainfalls caused a flash flood with devastating effect in the Elbe catchment area. Vast regions were flooded and 12 people died. Depending on the location, it corresponded to a flood with a mean return period of 50 to 500 years (Sächsisches Landesamt für Umwelt und Geologie (2004)). The physical damage to road infrastructure and bridges in Saxony amounted to 577 million Euros[6] (Leitstelle Wiederaufbau (2003), p.6ff) which corresponds to 9% of all physical damage[7]. After this event, the awareness for flood protection efforts increased throughout Germany. Baden-Wuerttemberg, for instance, now offers an online flood hazard map for selected river sections[8] and operates an early warning internet platform[9].

A non-weather-related potential cause for road disruptions in Baden-Wuerttemberg and throughout Germany are earthquakes. Baden-Wuerttemberg is one of the few areas in Germany where there is an actual earthquake risk, even though it is relatively low, compared to, for example, the subduction zone areas at the Pacific coasts. In Germany, the likely effects of

[6] Prices in 2002
[7] Residential and commercial buildings denoted the highest proportion of physical damage (Leitstelle Wiederaufbau (2003), p.2).
[8] http://www.uvm.baden-wuerttemberg.de/servlet/is/15783/# [12.8.2010]
[9] http://www.hvz.baden-wuerttemberg.de/ [12.8.2010]

earthquakes on roads are blocking debris due to infrastructure damages next to the road, landslides, as well as cracking or other damage to constructions like bridges. Figure 5 and Figure 6 depict the earthquake hazard, vulnerability and risk (residential buildings only) in Germany. The regions most prone to seismic risk are situated along the Rhine rift valley. The surroundings of Basel and the Swabian Alb in the southwest, West Saxony, and East Thuringia, as well as Cologne in the west of Germany experience the highest hazard levels.

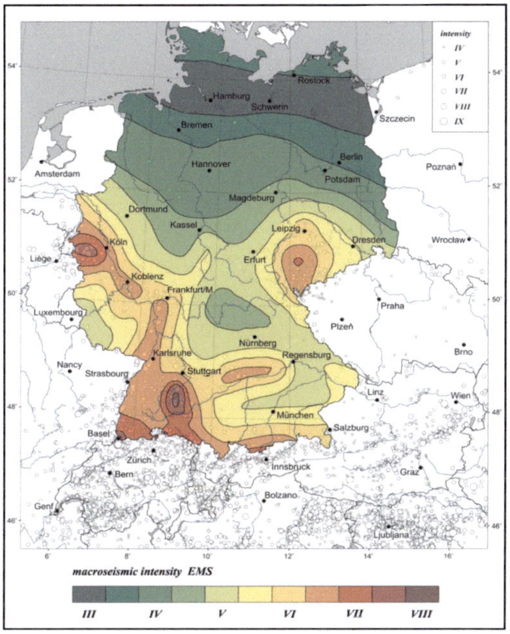

Figure 5: Earthquake hazard map for Germany for an exceedence probability of 0.0021 (equals a mean return period of 475 years) in terms of European Macroseismic Scale intensities[10] with epicenters of historical earthquakes in the background (Grünthal et al. (1998) cited in Grünthal (2004))

[10] See Table 18 in Chapter 6.1 for a more detailed description of this scale.

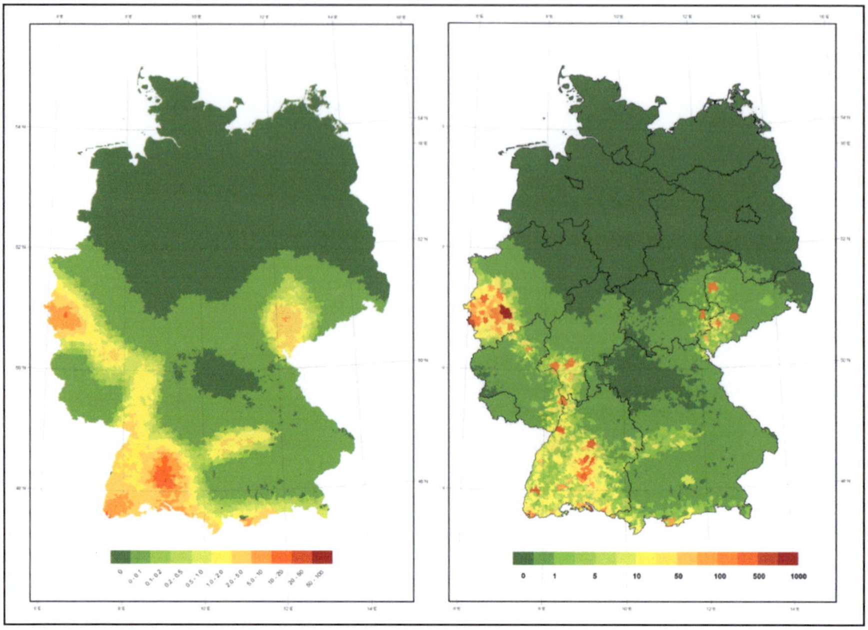

Figure 6: Estimated distribution of the mean seismic damage ratio [%] (left) and seismic risk [million €][11] (right) in German communities for an exceedence probability of 0.0021 (equals a mean return period of 475 years) (Tyagunov et al. (2006b))

TECHNICAL FAILURE/HUMAN ERRORS

The predominant cause of road closures are accidents, which are often triggered by human misbehavior or errors like drunkenness, aggressive driving style, speeding, tiredness and/or driving on the wrong side of the road. Technical failures of the infrastructure itself or the vehicles involved may also provoke accidents.

The collapse of the 8-lane Mississippi highway bridge on 1st August 2007 exemplifies what inadequate bridge design, insufficient inspection and the improper usage of technology may result in: 13 people died and 114 were injured (National Transportation Safety Board (2008)). It took more than a year to build a replacement bridge. A technical defect in a vehicle caused a serious incident in 1999, when a truck caught fire in the middle of the ca. 12 km long Montblanc tunnel due to a technical failure. 39 people died, 24 suffered injuries and the tunnel was closed for 3 years (Münchner Rückversicherungs-Gesellschaft (2003)).

Both examples provoked a better awareness of safety issues, and initiated technical and operational improvements beyond national borders. Although such prominent examples of tech-

[11] Prices in 2000

nical failures have not happened recently in Baden-Wuerttemberg, there is no immunity against these types of failure.

TERRORISM/CRIME

It is a common political goal to circumvent any criminal attack, no matter where it happens. Nevertheless, in the past decade, the mass transit system has repeatedly been a favored target of terroristic attacks as the examples in Moscow (2010), London (2005) and Madrid (2004) show. Although roads have not yet been the focus of maleficent acts, it is imaginable that major bridges or important tunnels may become targets in the future. It is hardly possible to prevent such an incident with measures like cameras or restricted access for pedestrians. Well-planned and organized disaster management may, however, contribute to keeping direct losses such as damages and casualties, and subsequently indirect losses, at a low level. Moreover, the physical effects of a terroristic attack may be comparable to other incidents such as fires or serious accidents, for which pre- or post-measures are often already in place or can be planned better.

2.2.2 DIRECT AND INDIRECT LOSS POTENTIAL

Authors specializing in risk research typically differentiate the potential negative consequences of an event into direct and indirect effects. Due to diverse methodological bases, mainly two different views exist concerning what these effects comprise.

CATEGORIZATION OF LOSSES

A large amount of publications use Computable General Equilibrium (CGE) models, Input-Output (I-O) models or social accounting matrices to calculate the losses associated with an unexpected event (e.g. Ho et al. (2001); Ellson et al. (1984); Brookshire et al. (1997)). They interpret direct and indirect losses behind this background. While the direct losses comprise the "direct change in production and demand due to the disruption of production facilities and lifelines from an unexpected event" (Ham et al. (2005b), p.850) indirect losses are defined as the "change in other sectors brought about by the change of a sector through input-output relationships" (ibid., p.850). In other words, the direct losses in this field of research are the losses a sector faces, when it is directly hit by an event (through, for example, business interruptions due to flooding) and the indirect losses occur through the interrelations (backward and forward linkages) between the sectors (e.g. supply shortages) (see Figure 7).

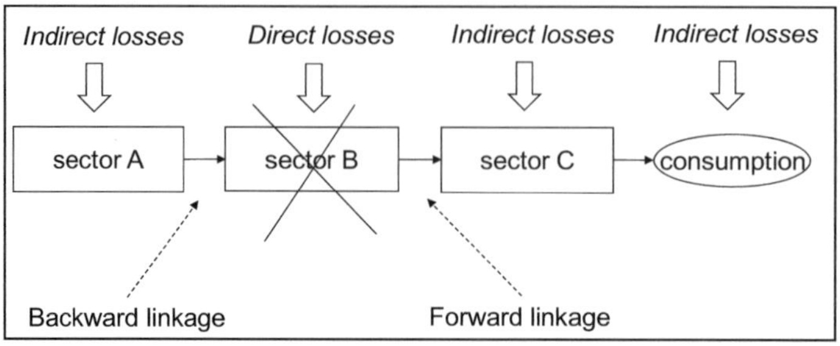

Figure 7: Exemplary illustration of I-O relationships and (in)direct losses (own illustration based on Van der Veen and Logtmeijer (2005))

The strong focus on industrial economic losses makes this categorization less generally applicable. Therefore this study interprets direct and indirect losses differently. Here, the distinction between direct and indirect losses follows the definitions provided in, for example, Mechler (2004), Meyer and Messner (2005), Green and Van der Veen (2007) and Khazai et al. (2011). Accordingly, direct losses refer to the physical damage or any other degrading effect on the condition of capital, human or other assets, including the costs of replacing and repairing damaged assets. Indirect losses are any impacts or losses triggered by the direct losses (Khazai et al. (2011)).

The physical vulnerability and the corresponding direct losses can be modelled in so-called fragility or damage functions ex-ante an event. They connect the intensity of an incident with the damage to an exposed element of a certain structure or building type. Damage functions for any kind of artifact are common in the seismic loss estimation literature (e.g. Applied Technology Council (ATC) (1991); Erdik and Fahjan (2006); Japan International Cooperation Agency (JICA) (2002); Shinozuka et al. (2000)). Regarding other hazards such as storms or flooding, damage functions generally focus on buildings (e.g. Heneka et al. (2006); Büchele et al. (2006)), but hardly include infrastructures such as roads or rail tracks (damaged, for example, by fallen trees or underwashing)[12]. Even if infrastructure damages cannot be estimated in full by damage functions, they can be considered an appropriate tool to estimate the direct loss potential of an event. This is particularly true in the case of earthquakes, but holds, to a minor extent, for other natural catastrophes as well. In the aftermath of an event, remote sensing has become an excellent tool for assessing the direct damage. The analysis of images be-

[12] This is most likely due to their rather complex interconnections, and the indifference of the insurance industry concerning public, non-insured goods.

fore and after an incident, together with a classification of elements and their mean value[13], can give a relatively quick impression of the direct economic losses. Furthermore the tool has proved to be helpful for immediate disaster assistance (e.g. Yamazaki (2001); Taubenböck et al. (2008)).

The introduced definitions of CI focus on the loss of function of the infrastructure, rather than on the physical damage an incident might entail. This is because in CI sectors a small amount of physical damage can entail enormous indirect losses. In the example of the power outage in 2006 given earlier, there was hardly any physical damage. The trigger to the incident was even intended and planned. However, nobody anticipated the extraordinary cascading effects and thereby caused indirect losses. Therefore it is the indirect loss potential that makes infrastructure a CI.

Indirect losses and road infrastructure

In respect to road infrastructure, the vulnerability concerning indirect losses alludes to the notions of serviceability, accessibility, robustness, resilience and/or reliability of a road/route/link.

The serviceability can be understood as "the basic ability of a system to deliver you from where you are, to where you want to be, at the time you want to travel, at a cost…that makes the journey worthwhile" (Goodwin (1992), p.661 quoted in Berdica (2002)). The concept of serviceability is the point of view from the supply side, as the correspondent to the notion of 'accessibility' from the demand side. Accessibility can be defined as the "ease with which activities may be reached from a given location" (Morris et al. (1979), p.91). The degradation of accessibility or serviceability due to an incident (like an accident or flooding of a road section) can be considered as the vulnerability in respect of indirect losses. Both concepts have a strong relationship with the terms 'resilience', 'robustness' and 'reliability', all of which are frequently used in the context of the vulnerability of a road network.

Resilience is often referred to as the "robustness of the system function and rapidity in its restoration if the function is impaired" (Shinozuka and Chang (2004), p.290). According to Holmgren (2007), robustness "signifies that the system will retain its system structure (function) intact (remains unchanged or nearly unchanged) when exposed to perturbations" (p.33f). Robustness and resilience may be treated as complements to vulnerability (Holmgren (2007), p.33). Reliability describes "the possibility to travel from one place to another" (Berdica

[13] An overview of typical values of transportation infrastructure elements can be found in ECLAC (2003), p.39.

(2002), p.120) and includes the probabilities of “at all reaching a chosen destination” (terminal reliability), “reaching a chosen destination in time” (travel time reliability) and “the network being able to ‘swallow’ a certain amount of traffic”(capacity reliability) (ibid.).

The notions of degraded serviceability of transportation networks presented in the last paragraphs are rather abstract. Hence, for defining the scope of this study in the context of CIs, a further differentiation of losses is necessary. The loss categories are delimited by the order of concernment by the disruption, respectively by the deepness of the cascading effects. The example in Figure 8 circumscribes the different orders of effects caused by a bridge damaged in an earthquake. The direct effects comprise the physical damage to the bridge. The indirect first order effects take into account evading actions related to bridge users that are immediately affected by the direct impact. Second order indirect effects concern those who bear the consequences of the first order impacts, and so on. It is crucial to explicitly declare the deepness of the effects under consideration. With increasing deepness, indirect effects become more complex, as, for example, positive impacts may counteract negative impacts. For example, due to foreseeable difficulties on the journey (e.g. a long detour or congestion caused by the bridge failure) a family changes its holiday destination. The original destination suffers losses over lost sales, while the new destination benefits from the altered plans. Effects can be considered as losses if their sum is negative.[14] The summation could be based on the monetary valuation of the effects, or on a qualitative list.

Categorization of effects	Example: earthquake damages bridge
Direct	**Physical damage** to bridge
Indirect 1st order	Bridge **users** have to make detours /change their plans due to direct effects on bridge
Indirect 2nd order	Customers, employers, familiy or others **related to bridge users** are affected by 1st order outcomes
Indirect 3rd order	Affected entities from the 2nd order effects cause **further consequences to other parties**
...	...

Figure 8: Categorization of effects of a disrupting event using the example of an earthquake-affected bridge

[14] If the sum of effects is positive, the effects may be called benefits.

2.3 INDIRECT LOSSES AND TRIP MAKING BEHAVIOR

Looking at the indirect effects of road closures mentioned in the previous chapter, it is the trip makers that experience the first order indirect losses. The impact on them determines the subsequent effects. Hence, it is of key interest how trip makers are affected in their journey and in their behavior in sudden degraded infrastructure conditions. The classical four-step approach to transport modeling accommodates the various trip making decision levels, and therefore helps to categorize possible effects. The approach was originally designed for passenger transport modeling but can, to a certain extent, also be applied to freight trip modeling. The following chapter explains these steps, and how these are typically modeled. Subsequently, empirical findings on trip making decisions during actual road disrupting events substantiate the comprehension of first order indirect effects caused by road disruptions.

2.3.1 MODELING OF TRIP MAKING BEHAVIOR: THE CLASSICAL FOUR-STEP APPROACH

The classical four-step algorithm related to (passenger) transport modeling traces back to transport modeling practices in the 1960s, and follows the reasoning of a sequential decision process (Ortuzar and Willumsen (2004), p.23). The first step is performed to decide on the number of trips that are generated in a region (trip generation). The second step distributes these trips to destinations (trip distribution). The transportation mode used to undertake the trips is determined in the third step (modal choice). Finally, all trips are assigned to routes (assignment). All steps require an underlying regional and network model as a basis. Figure 9 illustrates the four steps. Many freight transport modeling approaches also follow the principles of the four steps, but additionally include submodels to account for freight specific peculiarities e.g. the delivery lot size choice (e.g. Wisetjindawat et al. (2007)).

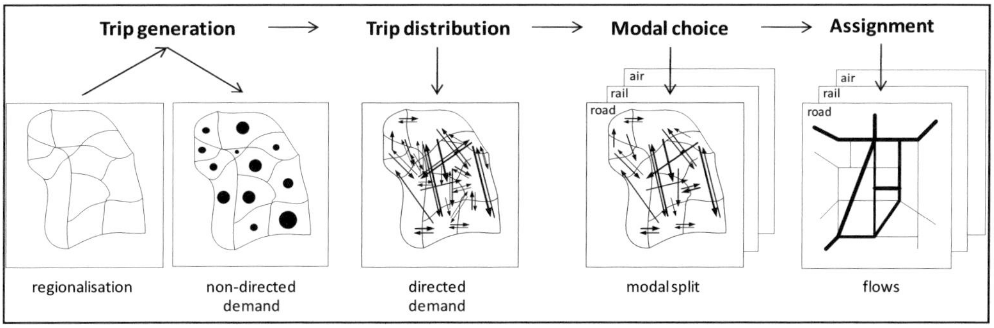

Figure 9: The four-step transport modeling approach (own illustration based on Hilty et al. (1996))

In a passenger transport demand model, the first step, the trip generation, models the number of trips that are undertaken by the population in a region. The trips can be classified by purpose, time of the day and trip maker type. Socioeconomic attributes, mainly car ownership and income level, have proven to influence the number of generated trips. One possible trip generation procedure groups the population into categories of specific socioeconomic characteristics such as age, gender, car ownership, or income, and assigns these categories trip rates based on the analysis of mobility studies (Ortuzar and Willumsen (2004)). In freight transport demand modeling, regression models are often used to derive the quantity of commodities produced and consumed (Ortuzar and Willumsen (2004); Wisetjindawat et al. (2007)).

In the following step the generated trips are distributed to their destinations. For both passenger and freight transport modeling, this may be performed in terms of an analogy to Newton's gravity law through the use of a gravity model, where two regions attract each other proportionally to their 'masses' and inversely proportional to their distance (Ortuzar and Willumsen (2004)). The masses correspond, for example, to the generated trips in one region (the origin) and the attractiveness of the targeted region (the destination). The 'distance' between the regions can include more components of the travel's disutility apart from the mere distance (e.g. duration, cost) (Wermuth (2005), p.274f).

Subsequently a logit model or another choice model serves for the calculation of the modal split for origin-destination pairs. A choice model determines the probability of an individual or a firm picking a certain mode for a specific origin-destination pair. This is usually based on the OD's particular range of transportation modes and their features such as cost, duration or convenience (Wermuth (2005), p.282). In freight transport modeling, the decision on shipment size determines to a great extent the mode choice, as every mode accommodates different types of shipments (e.g. palettes, containers) more or less adequately.

In the final step, the trips are assigned to the mode specific infrastructure. The route choice usually takes into account various cost components (e.g. duration, operational cost, tolls) captured in a generalized cost function of the available routes. Common approaches for the trip assignment considering capacity restraints comprise the user equilibrium (based on Wardrop's first principle[15]), stochastic user equilibrium, or the incremental assignment as approximation of the user equilibrium (Ortuzar and Willumsen (2004)). The Dijkstra algorithm offers one of

[15] "The journey times on all the routes actually used are equal, and less than those which would be experienced by a single vehicle on any unused route." (Wardrop (1952), p.345)

the most efficient methodologies to calculate the shortest (respectively cheapest) route in a network (Wermuth (2005), p.256), and thus is often used in the implementation of the assignment procedures. The decision on the assignment procedure is usually based on a balance between acceptable computation time and realistic traffic behavior.

All steps usually undergo a calibration procedure. Mobility surveys and traffic count data commonly serve for this purpose. The sequential structure of the decisions has often been substituted by simultaneous modeling of multiple steps (e.g. trip distribution and mode choice) or by changing the order of the steps (e.g. mode choice before destination choice) (Ortuzar and Willumsen (2004), p.25). One advantage of modeling the steps separately is an easy retrieval and interpretation of intermediate results which can be helpful in the calibration process. However, it lacks a behavioral interpretation as a whole, as all the steps are considered only by themselves and decision units may differ between steps. The classical approach may also fail in finding a unique equilibrium for all steps, but only for the individual ones (Oppenheim (1995), p.18). Despite these shortcomings, the classic four-step algorithm finds its practical application in passenger transport models throughout the world.

In past decades, disaggregated freight and passenger transport models have increasingly attracted the interest of researchers. In passenger demand modeling, activity-based simulation approaches build on the principle that travel demand is "treated as derived demand" (Jones (1979), p.77). Herein, a daily activity schedule with consideration of various constraints (e.g. time, budget) determines the travel demand (Ben-Akiva and Bowman (1998)). Microscopic freight transport modeling approaches have emerged rather recently. They try to incorporate logistic decisions and interactions between the main stakeholders in the distribution chain (e.g. shippers, carriers, forwarders, recipients) (Liedtke (2006); Hensher and Figliozzi (2007)). Generally, microscopic approaches have higher data requirements and hold more complexities than more aggregated approaches such as the ones embedded in a classical four step approach.

2.3.2 Road closures and trip making behavior: Empirical findings

The I-35W Mississippi bridge collapse in 2007 and other past events give interesting insights into the observed effects that a sudden closure of road sections can have on the trip making behavior of people and freight companies. Thus, they offer a solid foundation for the assumptions required in modeling indirect losses.

In their examination of 70 case studies and 200 expert opinions on roadspace reallocation, Cairns et al. (2002) identify as one of their key findings that "people react to a change in road conditions in much more complex ways than has traditionally been assumed in traffic models" (ibid, p.14). Changes in each of the four steps seem possible as a result of significant changes in roadspace reallocation according to a survey of transportation professionals (Cairns et al. (2002), p.19). Typically, changes in route choice have been assumed to be the prevalent adjustments in trip making behavior. Empirical studies confirm the importance of the rerouting in disrupting events (e.g. Gordon et al. (1998); Guiliano and Golob (1998)). For example, studies on the transport-related effects of the I-35W Mississippi bridge collapse in 2007 showed that 73% of the affected passenger car drivers adjusted their routing. But there were also 6% switching to another transportation mode and 61% changing their destination. Ca. 23% of the affected trip makers decided to cancel their trips or switch to telecommuting (Zhu et al. (2010), p.9)[16]. Other empirical studies summarized in Zhu and Levinson (2009) support these findings, assigning changes in the number of trips a minor, and changes in route choice and departure time a higher importance.

Surveys related to road closures caused by the Loma Prieta earthquake in 1989 and the Northridge earthquake in 1994 revealed similar observations with regard to freight transportation (Hansen and Sutter (1990), p.23; Willson (1998), p.47). Ca. 50-80% of the freight companies responded to the road closures with rerouting or rescheduling strategies (mainly to avoid congestion). Ca. 25-40% reduced their frequency of deliveries and pickups and/or increased their truck loads (ca. 30%). In the aftermath of the Loma Prieta earthquake ca. 40% of the truck companies stopped the service to certain areas. Mode shifts as one of the "longer term strategies" hardly happened (Willson (1998), p.42). Some effects, however, might not be caused directly by the road closures, but rather by demand shifts. For instance, after the Northridge earthquake 30% of the surveyed truck companies reported a gain and 15% a loss of customers (Willson (1998), p.41). Overall, freight companies demonstrated a high flexibility and ingenuity in their reactions after the earthquake. The disruptions were not considered as more extraordinary than other disruptions (e.g. strikes) they had been faced in the past (Willson (1998), p.47).

Case studies showed that the seriousness of road closure (partly or fully closed) and also the duration of the changed infrastructure conditions influence the level of change in transportation behavior (Cairns et al. (2002), p.17). The duration of closure has also been identified as

[16] Percentages of answers do not add up to 100% because multiple answers were possible.

an important factor by Willson (1998), Van der Veen (2003), as well as Lüders and Schulz (2010). It is also apparent that people might behave differently in an unusual setting than under normal conditions. For example, Tilahun and Levinson (2008) found out that after the I-35W Mississippi bridge collapse in 2007, affected people experimented with possible routes and tried two or more routes in the aftermath of the collapse to figure out the best one. Calculating with equilibrium conditions, as appropriate assignment procedure in normal situations, thus hardly reflects very realistic conditions immediately after the event.

Table 4 summarizes the main impacts of road disruptions on the travel behavior with regard to each of the four modeling steps based on the empirical findings.

Steps in transport modeling		impact on freight transportation		impact on passenger transportation	
First level	trip generation	low	stopped service	low	cancellation of trips
		high	rescheduling	high	departure time changes
		medium	reduced frequency/increased truck loads		
Second level	destination choice	*not mentioned*		medium	shift to available alternative destinations
Third level	modal choice	low	shift to available alternative modes	medium	shift to available alternative modes
Fourth level	route choice	high	rerouting	high	rerouting

Table 4: Impact of road disruptions on the travel behavior of people and freight companies with regard to each of the four classical modeling steps

2.4 Assessment of indirect losses due to road network degradation and the identification of critical road infrastructures

According to the definition of CI given in Chapter 1.1, it is the potential of indirect losses that make an infrastructure critical. Chapter 2.2.2 classified the indirect losses in losses of different orders. Since the focus of this study is on road infrastructure, the previous two chapters categorized the first order indirect effects according to the four steps in the classical transport model, and substantiated the effects with empirical findings of past road disrupting events.

In this chapter, state-of-the-art methodologies for the assessment of indirect losses due to road network degradation and the identification of critical road infrastructures are presented. The concepts may be subdivided in empirical surveys on indirect losses, approaches using a macroeconomic perspective, and approaches with a more network- and user-based perspective. Chapter 2.4.5 summarizes the characteristics of the concepts in a table.

2.4.1 Transport-related indirect losses based on empirical surveys

Empirical surveys on indirect losses associated with road disrupting events exist only for some selected incidents. In the aftermath of the Northridge Earthquake, which happened in 1994, some qualitative and quantitative surveys were carried out to identify and monetarily quantify all types of direct and indirect effects. The results of an extensive survey on the effects that businesses experienced after the earthquake, can be found in Tierney (1995) and Tierney (1997). Gordon et al. (1998) specifically explores the impact of business interruptions due to the road disruptions caused by the earthquake. The reported numbers of transport-related missed working days serve as input for the calculation of monetary losses within an I-O based model. Empirical surveys usually require high effort and funding shortly after an incident. The contacted and responding sample then determines significantly the quality of the results. The findings have to be interpreted in the context of the event's setting, restricting their transferability to other events and settings. Nevertheless, empirical surveys allow deep insights into the actual direct and indirect effects of an event, and may serve as an input for further calculations or models such as I-O models.

2.4.2 Transport-related indirect losses from a macroeconomic perspective

I-O and SCGE (Spatial Computable General Equilibrium) models are the most common methodologies for the quantification of indirect economic losses in literature (e.g. Cochrane (2004); Van der Veen and Logtmeijer (2005); Yamano et al. (2007)). The indirect losses here mainly contain the economic losses due to industrial interruptions. Okuyama (2007) and Okuyama (2009) give an overview on these methodologies, along with their advantages and drawbacks.

In order to be able to estimate the losses induced by infrastructure disruption, the models require an integrated transport model. This integration is rather difficult. For example, in I-O models, flows between industrial sectors are monetary in nature. Hence an infrastructure disruption first has to be translated into disrupted freight deliveries and production shortages on an aggregated sectoral level, and then has to be translated into monetary flows. A geographical matching of industrial production sites and I-O flows is hardly possible due to data restrictions and thus necessitates further modeling efforts. Therefore a coupling of an I-O table with a transport model is a rather complicated undertaking which requires a deep empirical foundation.

Research on the calculation of transportation-related losses based on I-O relationships has predominantly formed around two research clusters. Each group has one large integrated model for a specific region that can be applied to various scenarios. One of the clusters developed the Southern California Planning Model (SCPM and the follow up version of SCPM-2) for the area of Los Angeles and the calculation of earthquake losses. It is a combination of engineering models for the prediction of transportation infrastructure damage, a network equilibrium model (with the underlying road network) and an economic model (I-O model) for the prediction of spatial interactions and the propagating effects in the economy. The model has been applied to a hypothetical earthquake scenario in Elysian Park (e.g. Cho et al. (2001); Cho et al. (2000); Gordon et al. (2002)) and to the calculation of the transport-related business interruption effects resulting from an actual earthquake that happened in 1994 in Northridge (e.g. Gordon et al. (1998)).

The second cluster of researchers has built a combined model of interregional, multimodal commodity shipments and transportation network flows using an I-O model together with a transportation (highway) network model for the Midwest of the USA (e.g. Sohn et al. (2004); Ham et al. (2005a); Kim et al. (2002)). The losses are basically derived from the value of the mean shipment length increase (Ham et al. (2005b)). Beyond that, Sohn et al. (2003) analyze a set of 84 highway links against the background of an earthquake scenario using the potential economic impact when each single link is disrupted, and then rank them accordingly. They also calculate a normalized significance index of the links based on the ratio of the total cost increase due to the disruption, and the severity of the disruption (in the scenario). This index can be considered a criticality index, since it refers to the indirect loss potential of each link.

A combination of a transport model and an SCGE model has been suggested, for example, by Kim et al. (2004). An accessibility measure (based on distance between regions) serves as the connector between the two models. The authors analyze the impacts of investment in highway projects on macroeconomic indicators such as exports and consumption. Principally, their approach could also be applied to disinvestments, here corresponding to infrastructure disruptions.

Owing to the characteristics and assumptions of the I-O and the SCGE models, the estimated losses comprise indirect second order losses and beyond. Personal user costs and environmental effects due to detours are not considered. I-O models tend to overestimate the losses due to their inflexibility in substituting inputs and imports (Okuyama (2009)). Contrariwise, CGE models usually underestimate losses because they allow flexible adjustments (ibid). Both types of model are especially appropriate when it comes to capturing long-term macroeconomic effects caused, for example, by infrastructure disruptions.

2.4.3 *Identification of CIs: Topological Network measures and importance measures*

The criticality of network structures is the focus of Sakakibara et al. (2004), Grubesic and Murray (2006) and Albert and Barabási (2002). They analyze networks' robustness against failures, by applying topological network measures such as the 'clustering coefficient' or 'degree distribution'. One basic idea is, for instance, that a hub and spoke network is more prone to nodal failures than a less concentrated network. By classifying whole or partial networks into these categories, the measures can give a quick insight into the network's indirect loss potential. The defined boundaries of the network determine the results. These types of measure typically neglect network capacities, and do not allow deriving any concrete amount of expected losses or to categorize the losses more specifically.

From a network perspective, the identification of CIs could intuitively also be performed via the ranking of the annual average daily traffic (AADT) values on the roads under consideration (e.g. Schulz (2007)). Apart from traffic counts, this approach hardly requires any data or computation time. It neglects, however, the role and effect of redundancies in networks, and cannot quantify the effects in monetary terms.

The following concepts of importance and efficiency measures offer a more profound interpretation of the results. Both measures take into account network capacities and may be construed as first order indirect losses.

Jenelius et al. (2006) oppose the topological measures of Albert and Barabási (2002) to their own criticality measures (here: importance measures). Their three introduced concepts comprise the global importance of a road link (increase in travel cost per Origin Destination (OD) pair), the demand weighted importance (increase in travel cost per trip) and the relative unsatisfied demand due to the closure of a road section. Except for the latter, a monetary interpretation of the importance measures, and hence a translation into monetary indirect losses, is possible. The relative unsatisfied demand only refers to the demand originally travelling on the now disrupted link, neglecting possible destination or mode choice changes. Using the example of the northern Sweden road network, they take out one link after another and compare the generalized costs (here: non-monetized travel time between ODs on the shortest route) from all origins to all destinations, and compare these with the costs of the intact network[17].

---

[17] Tyagunov et al. (2007) applied the measures to the motorways and main roads in the federal state of Baden-Wuerttemberg in Germany.

In their case study, Jenelius et al. (2006) use only time as a cost measurement without monetization. The time component is undeniably the crucial factor for the determination of CIs. However, the monetization and differentiation by trip purpose influence the criticality as well. For example, 10 travelers on a private trip experiencing a 30 minute delay would suffer a loss of 25 Euro (assuming a value of time of 5 Euro/h for private travelers). If 5 of the travelers are on a business trip, the losses would rise to 62.5 Euro (when assuming a value of time of 20 Euro/h for business travelers). Neglecting the differentiation by purpose simplifies the calculation, but also neglects the individual valuation of additional travel time and therefore may under- or overestimate the severity of the indirect losses connected with specific road sections. The valuation of travel time hence plays a significant role in the indirect loss assessment, and consequently highly influences the criticality ranking.

The authors also suggest an indicator for the 'municipality exposure' which applies the three suggested criticality measures from the perspective of a region (aggregation of all origins inside the region to all destinations). The result of this study is a ranking of road links and municipalities in respect of the specific measures. Jenelius (2007a) and Jenelius (2010) extend this study with a detailed analysis in terms of regional equity in respect of municipality exposure. In complementary studies, the same author performs a regression analysis to explain the geographical disparities in municipality exposure, using indicators derived from public statistics (e.g. road density, population density), and takes into account the duration of the closure and the corresponding information level of road users with regard to the current road conditions (Jenelius (2007b); Jenelius (2009)).

Nagurney and Qiang (2007b) introduce an importance measure applicable to links and nodes. The measure is a further development of the ideas of Jenelius et al. (2006) and Latora and Marchiori (2004)[18]. An element is considered critical when its removal results in a large relative efficiency drop. A highly efficient network would serve high demand at low travel costs. The measure can be interpreted as the average (OD pair-based) performance (here: demand) vs. cost or price (here: travel time). Nagurney and Qiang apply their efficiency measure to a hypothetical power network and to a hypothetical road network with varying demand (Nagurney and Qiang (2008); Nagurney and Qiang (2007a)). Other authors adopt their methodology to the Baden-Wuerttemberg context (Tyagunov et al. (2007); Schulz (2007)). In their continuing work, Nagurney and Qiang also implement a network robustness index based on

[18] They originally suggested to calculate the efficiency drop in a network due to the loss of a node and applied it to a communication network.

their efficiency measure. For this purpose, they assume different degrees of network degradation throughout the network (Nagurney and Qiang (2007c)). In this context, they also suggest a relative total cost index for measuring a network's robustness (Nagurney and Qiang (2009)). The total costs consist of the links' free flow travel time multiplied by a penalty function due to congestion. The authors further expand their work with environmental considerations by proposing a link importance measure for the ranking of road links in respect of their environmental impact in the event of their removal (Nagurney et al. (2010)). The environmental impact corresponds to the relative increase in total CO emissions. All their measures forego the monetization issue, and therefore may appear rather abstract.

The importance and efficiency measures both focus on losses caused by rerouting. Except for the measure of relative unsatisfied demand, changes in trip generation, destination or mode choice remain unconsidered.

2.4.4 *Identification of CIs: Accessibility measures*

The impact on accessibility due to the capacity reduction in a road network can be considered as another criticality indicator based on first order indirect losses. The transition from the topological, efficiency or importance measures towards accessibility-based measures is very smooth. Taylor et al. (2006), Taylor and D'Este (2004) and Taylor and D'Este (2007) suggest three accessibility indices for the identification of critical road network elements. The first indicator calculates the loss of amenity due to a link disruption, which consists of the change in generalized costs between all ODs (here: travel time) multiplied by the demand between the ODs. The second index is the ARIA[19] index of remoteness. This is based on the road network distance from municipalities to the nearest service centers (categorized by their population as an approximation for the available services such as hospitals, education or banking). Hence, the index considers factors relevant for destination choice. This measure is especially suitable for scarcely populated regions. An extensive description of the ARIA index can be found in Commonwealth Department of Health and Aged Care (DHAC) (2001). The third proposed index is the Hansen integral accessibility index. For a specific region *i* the index is defined as the sum of each destination's attractiveness multiplied by their inverse travel distance from *i* and divided by the sum of the attractiveness of all destinations. The authors apply the measures to the main road network in Australia and compare the attractiveness results of each measure for selected links in an intact and in a disrupted network.

[19] **A**ccessability/**R**emoteness **I**ndex of **A**ustralia (ARIA)

Another accessibility measure is the 'logsum' which is often referred to in the field of transport modeling. The logsum derives from Discrete Choice Theory and can be interpreted as the expected maximum utility of an inhabitant of a specific region when undertaking a trip. A more detailed explanation on this concept can be found in Chapter 3.3.1. In contrast to the importance and efficiency measures, the logsum allows incorporating and monetizing changes in all trip-making decision steps. Berdica and Eliasson (2004), Chen et al. (2007), as well as Erath (2010), use the logsum in the vulnerability context of transportation networks. While Berdica and Eliasson (2004) mainly introduce the idea of the logsum's application in this field, Chen et al. (2007) and Erath (2010) also present the theoretical background and case studies. The case studies are set in a hypothetical network respectively in an area of 900 km² in Switzerland and result in an accessibility degradation value for each link. While Chen et al. (2007), like in many of the previously mentioned studies in the vulnerability context of roads, forego the monetization issue, Erath (2010) uses the marginal utility of income to express the accessibility changes in monetary terms.

2.4.5 Tabulated summary

The following table summarizes the described manifold concepts used to estimate indirect losses and to identify critical road infrastructures. For their specific purpose and scope of the assessment, the approaches are all appropriate.

However, the indirect effects assessed by the different concepts are never captured completely. Therefore a clear distinction as to what is explicitly and implicitly included in the indirect losses is crucial for the interpretation of the results. A better grasp of the results may be reached through monetization of the losses. This also serves for an easier communicability, especially when justifying risk management measures, and gives way to comparisons between different types of losses or other settings. Some of the presented approaches allow a monetary interpretation of the results. Others provide an index-based ranking which is, on the one hand, easy to understand in terms of what is more or less critical, but which may also appear rather abstract to, for example, politicians or the public in the event of defending public spending with regard to risk measures.

As CIs are commonly identified based on their indirect loss potential, the probabilities of failure and the risk in respect of a certain hazard are hardly ever mentioned. An exception is Jenelius (2009), who approximates probabilities of failure by the length of a road section. Probabilities and risk are not part of the CI definition. However, they provide useful information when evaluating the urgency associated with undertaking risk management measures and justifying them to the public.

As mentioned in Chapter 2.3.2, the duration of a road closure may influence the type and severity of the effects. An explicit differentiation of the effects by duration of closure can hardly be found. In his study, Jenelius (2007b) considers the postponement of a trip as a function of the duration of the closure. The empirical surveys take into account temporal aspects in the reported effects after the event.

None of the authors explicitly takes into account freight transportation changes due to disaggregated logistical decision alterations in terms of shipment size, delivery frequency, etc.

Most of the authors occupied with critical road infrastructure identification proceed by closing one individual road section after another, and comparing the new traffic assignment results with the conditions regarding an intact network. The road section with the highest negative differences is deemed to be the most critical. Due to network characteristics a simultaneous closure of multiple road sections may lead to complementary or substitutability effects. These cause either less or more losses compared to the sum of the individual closures' losses. Hence in the identification of CIs on the basis of expected indirect losses, this aspect needs to be considered. This is especially the case because realistic failure scenarios (such as a flood) usually affect more than one road section. However, this phenomenon has hardly ever been mentioned in the CI or the indirect loss literature.

Basic concept	Exemplary references	Advantages	Disadavantages	Assessment level	Type of losses	Type of rating (monetary, index)	Explicit differentiation by duration of closure	Differentiation by multiple and single road failures
Empirical surveys	• Tierney (1995) • Gordon et al. (1998)	• Deep insight in actual indirect and direct losses of an event • Findings may serve as input for further calculations or models (like I-O models)	• Empirical surveys usually require high efforts and funding shortly after an incident and sample determines significantly the results • Findings have to be interpreted in the context of the event's setting, restricting their transferability to other events and settings	• Businesses • Regional	All types of direct and indirect losses	index/ monetary	yes	no
Extended I-O	• Cho et al. (2001) • Gordon et al. (2002)	• Established and well accepted methodology for indirect loss calculation (> second order) based on industrial interrelationships • Relatively easy integration with other submodels	• First order indirect losses are not captured (e.g. additional user costs through detouring) • Tends to overestimate the losses • High data and calibration requirements and hence limited to certain regions	• National, state wide economy	Losses through industrial interrelationships, > Second order indirect losses	monetary	no	no
Extended SCGE	• Kim et al. (2004)	• Established and well accepted methodology for indirect loss calculation (> second order) based on market simulation	• Only long-run economic effects are captured • First order indirect losses are not captured (e.g. additional user costs through detouring) • Tends to underestimate the losses • High data and calibration requirements and hence limited to certain regions	• Multiregional economy	Losses in economic growth and regional disparities, > Second order indirect losses	monetary	no	no
Topological measures	• Albert and Barabási (2002) • Sakakibara et al. (2004) • Grubesic and Murray (2006)	• Quick and easy comparison of different networks possible concering their robustness against failures	• Network capacities usually neglected • Network definition crucial: where are the boundaries in the system? • Conclusions on concrete amount of losses not possible	• Network structure	No specific type of losses, but identification of network structures influencing robustness against failures and hence influencing indirect loss potential	index	no	no
Traffic counts	• Schulz (2007)	• Low data and computation time requirements	• Conclusions on concrete, absolute amount of losses not possible • Changes in trip generation, destination, mode or route choice neglected	• Network incl. users	Approximation of first order indirect losses	index	no	no
Importance measures	• Jenelius et al. (2006) • Jenelius (2007b)	• Index is possible to be monetized • Network capacities considered	• Changes in trip generation, destination or mode choice neglected	• Network incl. users • Regions	First and partly second order indirect losses	index/ monetary	yes	no
Efficiency measures	• Latora and Marchiori (2004) • Nagurney and Qiang (2007b)	• Network capacities considered	• Conclusions on concrete, absolute amount of losses not possible • Changes in trip generation, destination or mode choice neglected	• Network incl. users	First and partly second order indirect losses	index	no	no
Accessibility measures	• Taylor and D'Este (2007)	• One of the indices is possible to be monetarized • Changes in influencing factors for destination choice considered	• Changes in trip generation or mode choice neglected	• Network incl. users • Regions	First and partly second order indirect losses	index/ monetary	no	no
	• Berdica and Eliasson (2004) • Chen et al. (2007) • Erath (2010)	• Changes in route, destination and mode choice considered • Network capacities considered • Index is possible to be monetized	• High data and calibration requirements and hence limited to certain regions • Theoretical background is rather complicated to explain to somebody without economic or mathematical background	• Network incl. users • Regions • Users	First and partly second order indirect losses	index/ monetary	no	no

Table 5: Summary of the state-of-the-art methodologies in indirect loss estimation and CI identification

3 THE IDENTIFICATION OF CRITICAL ROAD INFRASTRUCTURES

3.1 CONDITIONS AND OBJECTIVES FOR THE IDENTIFICATION OF CI

The preceding chapters revealed that it is the potential effects caused by the loss of serviceability that make a CI critical. Therefore, the indirect loss potential determines the criticality of an infrastructure. It is hardly possible to account for all types of indirect losses with one methodology, as can be seen in the Table 5. The focus of this study is on critical road infrastructures. The immediate negative effects of a road disruption are the first order indirect losses. All other indirect losses are triggered by these. Through interactions on the road network, all directly affected road users add to the traffic on other roads, and potentially cause congestion which could further lead to the detouring of road users and consequently to higher indirect losses. These interactions are, strictly speaking, second order effects. In the short-run, the first order indirect losses dominate other types of losses. Due to its geographical and climatic setting in Germany, short interruptions due to floods, accidents or storms are most common. The criticality ranking of road infrastructures in this study is therefore based on first order indirect losses due to road disruptions, including second order losses through interactions with other road users. In other words, this study concentrates on the losses imposed on all trip makers in the network who are directly or indirectly affected by the closure.

Based on the identified strengths and weaknesses of the state-of-the-art methodologies for the identification of critical road infrastructures and indirect loss assessment as well as the context of CIs in respect to risk given in Chapter 2, this study aims to face the following challenges:

a) Develop a methodology for indirect loss assessment, incorporating changes on as many decision levels as possible and allowing a monetary interpretation, as a criticality measure for road network infrastructures
b) Differentiate the type of losses with regard to various time spans concerning the duration of road closure
c) Analyze the effects of simultaneous multiple road closures on the indirect loss and criticality assessment
d) Set the calculated indirect loss potential in the context of risk

The methodology and conditions associated with different durations of closure (objectives a) and b)) are presented in sections 3.2 and 3.3. Thereafter section 3.4 introduces the effects of multiple simultaneous road closures on the indirect loss and criticality assessment (objective c)) and relates these effects to the interdependencies with other type of infrastructure. Objective d), combining the indirect loss potential with probabilities of failure, only makes sense in a concrete context, and is therefore part of the case study, explained in more detail in Chapters 4 to 6. The Baden-Wuerttemberg case study further demonstrates how the suggested methodologies meet the identified challenges in a real geographical and network setting.

3.2 Determination of indirect short- and medium-term loss dimensions

Based on the empirical outcomes of the studies summarized in section 2.3.2, it is reasonable to assume route choice deviations including switching the departure time as the most common and immediate effect of road infrastructure disruptions. Changes in upper level decisions such as mode or destination choice usually require more organizational effort and affect the original travel decision in a more profound way. Modifications on the upper level are therefore assumed to be bound to a longer duration of disruption, so that more substantial decisions can be reassessed.[20] This leads to the following distinction of indirect losses due to infrastructure disruption:

- Short-term losses: In interrupting events taking three days or less[21], the indirect losses only comprise costs that occur due to changes in route choice.
- Medium-term losses: In events causing disruptions taking more than three days up to a few months, the indirect losses contain the short-term losses for the first three days. From the fourth day onwards the short-term losses are reduced by benefits arising by mode and/or destination choice changes as part of the evading strategies.

In severely disrupting events, that take more than a few months, it is very likely that political efforts lead to an upgrade of choice alternatives. This comprises, for example, an improved public transportation system with higher frequencies or a wider network, as happened after the 1994 Northridge earthquake in the wider area of Los Angeles (Guiliano and Golob (1998), p.4). Subsequent enhancements of the physically damaged sections, e.g. reopening of one lane, also alleviate the negative effects and therefore the losses. Thus, long-term losses are

[20] The same assumption was also taken by e.g. Erath et al. (2009), p.121.

[21] Three days or less are assumed to be a typical time span for short-term road interruptions caused by, for example, floods, storms or accidents with clean-up work in the geographical area of Germany.

dependent on activities concerning the handling of physical damage and other efforts to improve the transportation supply. Consequently, many factors influence the long-run development of network and behavioural conditions. Since they are not the focus of this study, the time span considered here is restricted to up to a few months. Considering the empirical insights mentioned in section 2.3.2, changes in the trip generation, suppressing or increasing the number of undertaken trips are negligible compared to the other choice levels, and are hence not incorporated in the indirect losses here. They could, however, easily be integrated into the medium-term losses, as the calculation technique would basically stay the same.

Furthermore, due to limited data access for the purpose of this study, changes in mode choice cannot be incorporated in the later demonstrated case study. The medium-term loss calculations therefore concentrate only on trip distribution changes, assuming an inelastic mode choice. In accordance with the trip generation, the mode choice could easily be incorporated into the loss calculation methodology.

Trip specific choice elasticities are dependent on the purpose of the trip. While freight traffic, commuters and travelers on business trips can hardly change their destination in the short- and medium-term flexibly, travelers on private trips such as shopping or leisure activities may easily switch their destination (Erath (2010), p.9). Therefore predominantly private trip makers have the potential to reduce the expected daily losses of detouring by additional choice changes. This study hence limits the calculation of the medium-term effects to private trips. The methodology would stay the same, if business or commuter trips were considered. Due to varying elasticities, all trip purposes would, however, require separate model specifications. If the impact on freight traffic was to be assessed in more detail, the suggested methodology for medium-term losses would have to be substituted by freight-specific transport models, which also consider changes in tour-plans, lot size, etc. (as suggested by, for example, Wisetjindawat et al. (2007) for an urban surrounding) and allow a monetary assessment of the altered situation.

Taking into account the conditions of short- and medium-term losses as just mentioned, the following paragraphs first explain the rationale behind the indirect loss calculation as a basis for the CI identification and then the methodology itself. A simple example then demonstrates the application of the methodology.

3.3 The calculation of indirect short- and medium-term losses

The logsum measure, which has also been suggested by, for example, Chen et al. (2007) and Erath (2010), as part of a nested logit transport model fulfills most of the requirements set for the purpose of this study. In contrast to the classical four step approach with different models in each step, a nested logit transport model is closer to human decision making. The retrievable logsum measure is able to take into account changes in all trip decision steps, and allows an economic interpretation in monetary terms. The measure further offers an analysis of indirect losses, not only based on a network's link, but also on a regional basis (e.g. which region is most affected by an infrastructure disruption?). The following paragraphs explain the rationale behind the logsum measure, and derive its application for indirect loss assessment.

3.3.1 The logsum measure and its background in discrete choice theory

The logsum measure, in this context also called EMU (expected maximum utility), originates from discrete choice theory and the concept of random utility. Assuming that there are known, measurable as well as random parts in the utility a decision maker gains from choosing an option *o* in an alternative set *A*, the utility is (e.g. McFadden (1974)):

$$U_o = V_o + \varepsilon_o \quad \forall o \tag{3-1}$$

U_o *utility of alternative o*

V_o *known, measurable part of utility*

ε_o *random part of utility*

The observable part of the utility function V_o consists of decision-relevant characteristics of an option. In the context of travel mode choice this is, for example, the duration of the trips concerned. The random term ε_o accounts for unobserved attributes, taste variations, measurement errors, imperfect information and instrumental variables (Manski (1973), p.13f). ε_o is assumed to be independent from other alternatives and to follow a Gumbel distribution. Based on this presupposition it is possible to reformulate the probability to choose *o* over all other alternatives $b \in A$ (Ben-Akiva and Lerman (1985))

$$P_o = P_o(V_o + \varepsilon_o > V_b + \varepsilon_b \,, \forall b \neq o) \tag{3-2}$$

into the well known formula (e.g. McFadden (1974); Ortuzar (1982); Ben-Akiva and Lerman (1985); Train (2003))

$$P_o = \frac{e^{\alpha V_o}}{\sum_{b \in A} e^{\alpha V_b}} \tag{3-3}$$

with alpha being reciprocal to the standard deviation σ of the random term distribution

$$\alpha = \frac{\pi}{\sqrt{6}\sigma} \tag{3-4}$$

In case alpha is zero, the probability of choosing alternative *o* is *1/A*. A very high alpha sets the probability close to one for the alternative with the highest *V* and near to zero for all other alternatives.

A utility maximizing individual faced with the alternative set A may expect to receive the following utility in the form of a 'logsum'

$$E\left[\max_{o \in A}(U_o)\right] = EMU = \frac{1}{\alpha} \ln \sum_{o \in A} e^{\alpha V_o} + const \tag{3-5}$$

EMU *Expected maximum utility of an alternative set A*

const *Constant*

The constant accounts for utility components which further contribute to the absolute value of utility, e.g. decision-irrelevant components left out in U_o. The constant is hence only a crucial part of the formula, when absolute values of utility are of relevance. It is, however, negligible when calculating changes in the EMU (de Jong et al. (2007), p.876).

In a nested logit approach, decisions are set in a hierarchical order. Its application is especially adequate if there are alternatives with similar characteristics that can be partitioned into subsets. The decision steps in a transport model allow such a partition as depicted in Figure 10. Individual travelers are assumed to choose among travel alternatives (travel, destination, mode, route) by maximizing their utility (Oppenheim (1995), p.27f).

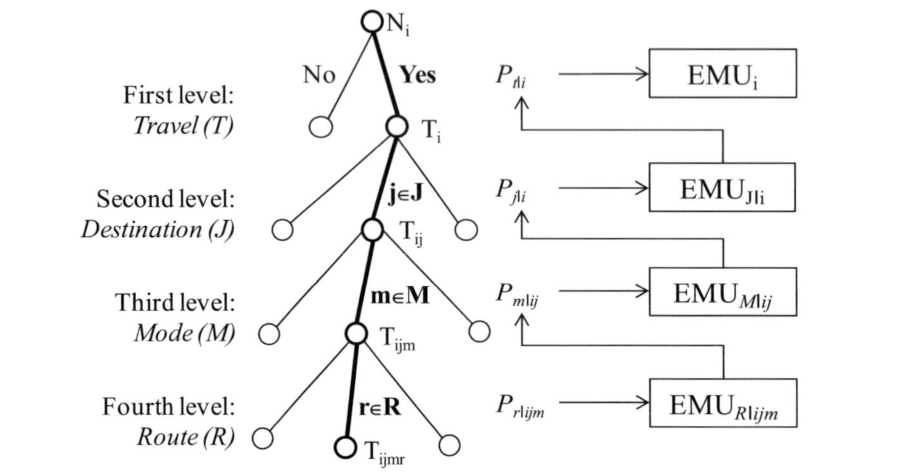

N_i is the potential travellers in origin $i \in I$

$\boldsymbol{P_{tli}}$ is the probability of making a trip given N_i

$\boldsymbol{T_i} = N_i P_{tli}$ is the travel demand in origin $i \in I$

$\boldsymbol{P_{jli}}$ is the probability of choosing desination $j \in J$ given T_i

$\boldsymbol{T_{ij}} = T_i P_{jli}$ is the travel demand from origin $i \in I$ to destination $j \in J$

$\boldsymbol{P_{mlij}}$ is the probability of choosing mode $m \in M$ given T_{ij}

$\boldsymbol{T_{ijm}} = T_{ij} P_{mlij}$ is the travel demand from origin $i \in I$ to destination $j \in J$ on mode $m \in M$

$\boldsymbol{P_{rlijm}}$ is the probability of choosing route $r \in R$ given T_{ijm}

$\boldsymbol{T_{ijmr}} = T_{ijm} P_{rlijm}$ is the travel demand taking route $r \in R$ from origin $i \in I$ to destination $j \in J$ on mode $m \in M$

EMU$_{\mathbf{i}}$ is the expected maximum utility in origin $i \in I$

EMU$_{\mathbf{Jli}}$ is the expected maximum utility in origin $i \in I$ from travelling

EMU$_{Mlij}$ is the expected maximum utility when travelling from origin $i \in I$ to destination $j \in J$

EMU$_{Rlijm}$ is the expected maximum utility when travelling from origin $i \in I$ to destination $j \in J$ with mode $m \in M$

Figure 10: Hierarchical structure of a combined transport model (own illustration based on Chen et al. (2007), p.246, Yao and Morikawa (2005), p.371, and Oppenheim (1995), p.20)[22]

The EMUs retrievable on each step go into the conditional probabilities to choose a specific alternative on the precedent step, resulting in the following terms (e.g. Chen et al. (2007), p.274):

Fourth level (route (r)):
$$P_{\text{rl}ijm} = \frac{e^{\alpha_R V_{ijmr}}}{\sum_{k \in R} e^{\alpha_R V_{ijmk}}} \;\forall i, j, m, \text{r} \tag{3-6}$$

Third level (mode (m)):
$$P_{\text{ml}ij} = \frac{e^{\alpha_M (V_{ijm} + \text{EMU}_{\text{Rl}ijm})}}{\sum_{l \in M} e^{\alpha_M (V_{ijl} + \text{EMU}_{Rlijm})}} \;\forall i, j, m \tag{3-7}$$

$$\text{EMU}_{Rlijm} = \frac{1}{\alpha_R} \ln \sum_{r \in R} e^{\alpha_R V_{ijmr}} + const_R \;\forall i, j, m \tag{3-8}$$

---

[22] N_i as the potential travelers in region i correspond to the potential trip making decisions generated in this region. It can be derived by dividing the number of daily trips generated in region i (retrieved, for example, from mobility studies) with the probability of making a trip P_{tli}.

Second level (destination (j)): $$P_{\mathrm{j|i}} = \frac{e^{\alpha_J(V_{ij}+\mathrm{EMU}_{M|ij})}}{\sum_{n\epsilon J} e^{\alpha_J(V_{in}+\mathrm{EMU}_{M|ij})}} \, \forall i,j \qquad (3\text{-}9)$$

$$\mathrm{EMU}_{M|ij} = \frac{1}{\alpha_M} \ln \sum\nolimits_{m\in M} e^{\alpha_M(V_{ijm}+\mathrm{EMU}_{R|ijm})} + const_M \, \forall i,j \qquad (3\text{-}10)$$

First level (travel (t))[23]: $$P_{\mathrm{i|t}} = \frac{e^{\alpha_I(V_i+\mathrm{EMU}_{J|\mathrm{i}})}}{1+e^{\alpha_I(V_i+\mathrm{EMU}_{J|\mathrm{i}})}} \forall i \qquad (3\text{-}11)$$

$$\mathrm{EMU}_{J|\mathrm{i}} = \frac{1}{\alpha_J} \ln \sum\nolimits_{j\in J} e^{\alpha_J(V_{ij}+\mathrm{EMU}_{M|ij})} + const_J \, \forall i \qquad (3\text{-}12)$$

$$EMU_i = \frac{1}{\alpha_i} \ln(1 + e^{\alpha_i(V_i+\mathrm{EMU}_{J|\mathrm{i}})}) + const_i \, \forall i \, . \qquad (3\text{-}13)$$

EMU_i, $EMU_{J|i}$, $EMU_{M|ij}$, $EMU_{R|ijm}$: Expected maximum utilities

$const_R$, $const_M$, $const_J$, $const_I$: Constants

Since in a nested logit model the variance of the consumers' valuation between sub-alternatives should generally be smaller than the variance in decisions on the level above, alpha increases with the deepth of a decision in a nest. In a nested transport model, the alpha in respect to the utility a consumer gets from, for example, route choice is higher than the alpha connected to the mode choice decision.

3.3.2 THE LOGSUM MEASURE AS AN ACCESSIBILITY MEASURE AND ITS ECONOMIC INTERPRETATION

The EMU of one decision step can be interpreted as an accessibility measure as it is "the expected 'worth' of a subset of travel alternatives" (Ben-Akiva and Lerman (1985), p.301). The worthiness of a consumption decision from the point of view of a person can be expressed in the consumer surplus (CS). The CS of a person is the monetized utility received by this person in the choice situation (Train (2003), p.59). A monetized EMU of a choice hence can be considered as the CS[24]. In order to calculate the CS of, for example, a region, the CS of each choice (the EMU) has to be multiplied by the number of decisions taken in this region. The difference in consumer surplus (ΔCS) of an individual in two settings, for example, before and after a road closure, corresponds to the difference of the monetized EMUs of the settings.

[23] The utility from not travelling at all is assumed to be zero.

[24] The EMU may further be interpreted as the integral of a demand curve provided that the choice probability is the expected demand (de Jong et al. (2005), p.10). In a nested logit model the lower nests thus have conditional demand curves (given the decisions above).

Multiplying the individual ΔCS with the number of decision making units results in the total ΔCS.

There are various ways to monetize the EMUs (Ben-Akiva and Lerman (1985), p.304). If the utility is expressed in monetary terms already, a later monetization is not necessary, as the EMU is already in monetary units[25]. No matter how and when the monetization takes place, it will always provoke criticism, especially with regard to the valuation of time. As there are various ways to conduct the monetization with different degrees of complexity and coarseness, it is crucial to explain clearly where the numbers come from in order to ensure traceability and credibility. The monetizing procedure for the case study will be discussed in more detail in Chapter 4.3.

The utility a decision maker obtains by a choice may be explained in terms of cost, respectively negative utility. Then the exponents in the conditional probabilities become negative so that higher costs of an alternative lower the choice probability. The EMUs can also be expressed in a negative form, reflecting the expected minimal costs or disutility rather than the expected maximal utility from a subset of alternatives.

3.3.3 *THE APPLICATION OF THE LOGSUM MEASURE FOR INDIRECT SHORT- AND MEDIUM-TERM LOSS ASSESSMENT*

The following sections describe the calculation of short- and medium-term losses based on CS changes for a time span of one day. As just mentioned, the difference of two monetized EMUs is the consumer surplus change per decision taken. Assuming an inelastic travel demand, the consumer surplus change $\Delta CS_{/\!\!\!\!\Lambda i}$ in region i caused by a road disruption is then:

$$\Delta CS_{/\!\!\!\!\Lambda i} = O_i(\widetilde{EMU}_{JIi} - EMU_{JIi}) \qquad (3\text{-}14)$$

$\Delta CS_{/\!\!\!\!\Lambda i}$ *Consumer surplus change assuming an inelastic travel demand in region i*

O_i *Trips generated in region i*

$\widetilde{EMU}_{JIi}$ *Expected maximum utility of making a trip originating in region i in case of a disrupted road network*

EMU_{JIi} *Expected maximum utility in case of an intact road network*

[25] $[U] = € \Rightarrow [\varepsilon] = € \Rightarrow [\sigma] = € \Rightarrow [\alpha] = \frac{1}{€} \Rightarrow [EMU] = €$

The basis for the EMU calculations poses a demand-constrained model for trip distribution and is typically formulated as follows (Wermuth (2005), p.280):

$$P_{j|i} = \frac{A_j e^{-\alpha_J c_{ij}}}{\sum_{n\epsilon J} A_n e^{-\alpha_J c_{in}}} = \frac{e^{\alpha_J \frac{lnA_j}{\alpha_J} - \alpha_J c_{ij}}}{\sum_{n\epsilon J} e^{\alpha_J \frac{lnA_n}{\alpha_J} - \alpha_J c_{in}}} \tag{3-15}$$

$$T_{ij} = O_i \frac{A_j e^{-\alpha_J c_{ij}}}{\sum_{n\epsilon J} A_n e^{-\alpha_J c_{in}}} \tag{3-16}$$

$$EMU_{J|i} = \frac{1}{\alpha_J} ln \sum_{j\in J} A_j e^{-\alpha_J c_{ij}} + const_J \tag{3-17}$$

$P_{j|i}$ *Probability of choosing destination j coming from origin i*

T_{ij} *Number of trips between origin i and destination j*

A_j *Measure of the attractiveness of region j (e.g. number of attractive locations, population) – may be interpreted as part of the utility and/or as a weighting factor for the number of attractive locations at the destination*

c_{ij} *Expected costs (here: generalized costs) for going from i to j considering all transport modes (e.g. operational costs, time costs) corresponding to $EMU_{M|ij}$ (or $EMU_{R|ijm}$ in case mode choice is neglected)*

For the purpose of calculating changes in EMUs and CS, the constant $const_J$ may be neglected.

For simplification, first an increase of the costs only of going from one specific region i to region j is assumed, so that:

$$\tilde{c}_{ij} = c_{ij} + \Delta c_{ij} \tag{3-18}$$

This consequentially leads to a variation of the expected maximum utility (Taylor approximated):

$$\widetilde{EMU}_{J|i} = EMU_{J|i} + \frac{\partial EMU_{J|i}}{\partial c_{ij}} \Delta c_{ij} + \frac{1}{2} \frac{\partial^2 EMU_{J|i}}{\partial c_{ij}^2} \Delta c_{ij}^2 + \ldots$$

$$\frac{\partial EMU_{J|i}}{\partial c_{ij}} = \frac{1}{\alpha_J} \frac{1}{\sum_{n\epsilon J} A_n e^{-\alpha_J c_{in}}} (-\alpha_J) A_j e^{-\alpha_J c_{ij}} = -\frac{A_j e^{-\alpha_J c_{ij}}}{\sum_{n\epsilon J} A_n e^{-\alpha_J c_{in}}}$$

$$\frac{\partial^2 EMU_{Jli}}{\partial c_{ij}^{\ 2}} = -\frac{(-\alpha_J)A_j e^{-\alpha_J c_{ij}} \sum_{n\epsilon J} A_n e^{-\alpha_J c_{in}}}{\left(\sum_{n\epsilon J} A_n e^{-\alpha_J c_{in}}\right)^2} + \frac{A_j e^{-\alpha_J c_{ij}} (-\alpha_J) A_j e^{-\alpha_J c_{ij}}}{\left(\sum_{n\epsilon J} A_n e^{-\alpha_J c_{in}}\right)^2}$$
$$= \frac{\alpha_J A_j e^{-\alpha_J c_{ij}}}{\sum_{n\epsilon J} A_n e^{-\alpha_J c_{in}}} - \frac{\alpha_J A_j^{\ 2} e^{-2\alpha_J c_{ij}}}{\left(\sum_{n\epsilon J} A_n e^{-\alpha_J c_{in}}\right)^2}$$

$$\widetilde{EMU}_{Jli} = EMU_{Jli} - \frac{A_j e^{-\alpha_J c_{ij}}}{\sum_{n\epsilon J} A_n e^{-\alpha_J c_{in}}} \Delta c_{ij} + \frac{1}{2} \frac{\alpha_J A_j e^{-\alpha_J c_{ij}}}{\sum_{n\epsilon J} A_n e^{-\alpha_J c_{in}}} \Delta c_{ij}^{\ 2} - \frac{1}{2} \frac{\alpha_J A_j^{\ 2} e^{-2\alpha_J c_{ij}}}{\left(\sum_{n\epsilon J} A_n e^{-\alpha_J c_{in}}\right)^2} \Delta c_{ij}^{\ 2} + \ldots \tag{3-19}$$

The fourth term on the right hand side, with its exponentiated denominator, is very small compared to the preceding terms. The subsequent terms become even smaller. These small terms contribute to more precise results but also to more complex calculations. For the purpose of this study, these terms are therefore neglected, and the altered accessibility in region *i* is then:

$$\widetilde{EMU}_{Jli} = EMU_{Jli} - \frac{A_j e^{-\alpha_J c_{ij}}}{\sum_{n\epsilon J} A_n e^{-\alpha_J c_{in}}} \Delta c_{ij} + \frac{1}{2} \frac{\alpha_J A_j e^{-\alpha_J c_{ij}}}{\sum_{n\epsilon J} A_n e^{-\alpha_J c_{in}}} \Delta c_{ij}^{\ 2} \tag{3-20}$$

Before interpreting this term, now a change in costs coming from region *i* going to **all** regions *j* is assumed, so that

$$\tilde{c}_{ij} = c_{ij} + \Delta c_{ij} \ \ \forall j \in J \tag{3-21}$$

results in the following new accessibility (Taylor approximated):

$$\widetilde{EMU}_{Jli} = EMU_{Jli} - \frac{A_j e^{-\alpha_J c_{i1}}}{\sum_{n\epsilon J} A_n e^{-\alpha_J c_{in}}} \Delta c_{i1} - \frac{A_j e^{-\alpha_J c_{i2}}}{\sum_{n\epsilon J} A_n e^{-\alpha_J c_{in}}} \Delta c_{i2} - \cdots + \frac{1}{2} \frac{\alpha_J A_j e^{-\alpha_J c_{i1}}}{\sum_{n\epsilon J} A_n e^{-\alpha_J c_{in}}} \Delta c_{i1}^{\ 2} +$$
$$\frac{1}{2} \frac{\alpha_J A_j e^{-\alpha_J c_{i2}}}{\sum_{n\epsilon J} A_n e^{-\alpha_J c_{in}}} \Delta c_{i2}^{\ 2} + \ldots^{***} - \frac{1}{2} \frac{\alpha_J A_j^{\ 2} e^{-2\alpha_J c_{i1}}}{\left(\sum_{n\epsilon J} A_n e^{-\alpha_J c_{in}}\right)^2} \Delta c_{i1}^{\ 2} -$$
$$\frac{1}{2} \frac{\alpha_J A_j^{\ 2} e^{-2\alpha_J c_{i2}}}{\left(\sum_{n\epsilon J} A_n e^{-\alpha_J c_{in}}\right)^2} \Delta c_{i2}^{\ 2} - \ldots - 2 \frac{\alpha_J A_1 A_2 e^{-\alpha_J c_{i1}} e^{-\alpha_J c_{i2}}}{\left(\sum_{n\epsilon J} A_n e^{-\alpha_J c_{in}}\right)^2} \Delta c_{i1} \Delta c_{i2} -$$
$$2 \frac{\alpha_J A_1 A_3 e^{-\alpha_J c_{i1}} e^{-\alpha_J c_{i3}}}{\left(\sum_{n\epsilon J} A_n e^{-\alpha_J c_{in}}\right)^2} \Delta c_{i1} \Delta c_{i3} - \ldots - 2 \frac{\alpha_J A_2 A_3 e^{-\alpha_J c_{i2}} e^{-\alpha_J c_{i3}}}{\left(\sum_{n\epsilon J} A_n e^{-\alpha_J c_{in}}\right)^2} \Delta c_{i2} \Delta c_{i3} -$$
$$2 \frac{\alpha_J A_2 A_3 e^{-\alpha_J c_{i2}} e^{-\alpha_J c_{i4}}}{\left(\sum_{n\epsilon J} A_n e^{-\alpha_J c_{in}}\right)^2} \Delta c_{i2} \Delta c_{i4} - \ldots \tag{3-22}$$

Again, all the terms after the term *** are neglected. Thus[26]:

$$\widetilde{EMU}_{JIi} = EMU_{JIi} - \sum_{j\in J} \frac{A_j e^{-\alpha_J c_{ij}}}{\sum_{n\in J} A_n e^{-\alpha_J c_{in}}} \Delta c_{ij} + \frac{1}{2}\alpha_J \sum_{j\in J} \frac{A_j e^{-\alpha_J c_{ij}}}{\sum_{n\in J} A_n e^{-\alpha_J c_{in}}} \Delta c_{ij}^{\,2} \quad (3\text{-}23)$$

$\widetilde{EMU}_{JIi}$ consists of the original EMU_{JIi} (in an intact network) diminished by the changes in costs between the regions caused by the road closure multiplied by the trip making probability between these regions. This deduction is attenuated by a further term which can be interpreted as a destination choice change induced loss reductor.

The short-term losses *STL* and medium-term losses *MTL* with regard to CS changes due to a closure of a section *s* can then be formulated in the following way:

$$\mathrm{STL_s} = \sum_{i\in I} O_i \left(\left[\mathrm{EMU_{JIi}} - \sum_{j\in J} \frac{A_j e^{-\alpha_J c_{ij}}}{\sum_{n\in J} A_n e^{-\alpha_J c_{in}}} \Delta c_{ij}\right] - \mathrm{EMU_{JIi}}\right) =$$

$$-\sum_{i\in I}\left(O_i \sum_{j\in J} \frac{A_j e^{-\alpha_J c_{ij}}}{\sum_{n\in J} A_n e^{-\alpha_J c_{in}}} \Delta c_{ij}\right) = -\sum_{i\in I}\sum_{j\in J} T_{ij}\Delta c_{ij} = \sum_{i\in I}\sum_{j\in J} \Delta CS_{RIijm}{}^{27} \quad (3\text{-}24)$$

$$\mathrm{MTL_s} = \sum_{i\in I} \Delta CS_{JIi} = \sum_{i\in I} O_i \left(\widetilde{\mathrm{EMU}}_{\mathrm{JIi}} - \mathrm{EMU_{JIi}}\right) = \sum_{i\in I}\left(O_i \left[-\sum_{j\in J} \frac{A_j e^{-\alpha_J c_{ij}}}{\sum_{n\in J} A_n e^{-\alpha_J c_{in}}} \Delta c_{ij} + \right.\right.$$

$$\left.\left.\frac{1}{2}\alpha_J \sum_{j\in J} \frac{A_j e^{-\alpha_J c_{ij}}}{\sum_{n\in J} A_n e^{-\alpha_J c_{in}}} \Delta c_{ij}^{\,2}\right]\right) = -\sum_{i\in I}\sum_{j\in J} T_{ij}\,\Delta c_{ij} + \sum_{i\in I} O_i \frac{1}{2}\alpha_J \sum_{j\in J} \frac{A_j e^{-\alpha_J c_{ij}}}{\sum_{n\in J} A_n e^{-\alpha_J c_{in}}} \Delta c_{ij}^{\,2}$$

(3-25)

The MTL_s summed up over all regions *i* hence contains the STL_s, the detouring costs, and a term reducing these losses by reasonable destination choice changes. The MTL_s and STL_s are the same, if the quadratic term in the Taylor development of the accessibility cost formula is very small, formally: $\frac{1}{2}\alpha_J \Delta c_{ij}^{\,2} \rightarrow 0 \ \forall j \in J$.

The term 'losses' here refers to the negative changes in CS. Strictly speaking, negative changes in CS are positive losses. Therefore, the negative outcome of the formulas corresponds actually to the negative changes in CS and not to negative losses (= gains). This has to be considered when interpreting the results. To avoid confusion, with regard to the Baden-Wuerttemberg case study later on, losses are expressed positively although negative CS changes pose their basis.

[26] The same calculation could also be done for the valuation of changes in $\mathrm{EMU_{MIi}}$ triggered by changes in $\mathrm{EMU_{RIijm}}$ (here: Δc_{ijm}). The outcome is the same with the corresponding indices of the mode decision step.

$$\widetilde{EMU}_{MIij} = EMU_{MIij} - \sum_{m\in M} \frac{e^{-\alpha_M c_{ijm}}}{\sum_{l\in M} e^{-\alpha_M c_{ijl}}} \Delta c_{ijm} + \frac{1}{2}\alpha_M \sum_{m\in M} \frac{e^{-\alpha_M c_{ijm}}}{\sum_{l\in M} e^{-\alpha_M c_{ijl}}} \Delta c_{ijm}^{\,2}$$

[27] The latter identity holds only for *m* being a constant. This is the case if only one mode is available in the network under consideration or if mode changes are negligible.

One of the advantages of the suggested approach is that short- and medium-term losses are captured in one single monetary measure. There is no necessity to recalculate all transport modeling steps. Here, except for reassigning the trips on the network and calculating the costs associated with the network assignment, no other step has to be fully recalculated. In the event that mode choice and trip generation are not assumed to react inelastically with regard to road closures, the interpretation of short- and medium-term losses would vary, but the principal procedure to assess the losses by approximating them with one single measure is still valid.

If only short-term losses (route choice changes) are of relevance, a logit model is not necessarily required. How the OD matrices were developed is then not important since no adjustment and no valuation of mode/destination choice are considered.

As already mentioned in Chapter 3.2, this study neglects changes in trip generation. Losses induced by trip cancellations are retrievable through CS changes on the trip generation level. A variation of departure time does not change the consumer surplus, as long as the departure time stays within the time span the model represents. However, changing the time span (e.g. to an hourly instead of a daily basis) or incorporating different departure times into the trip destination, mode choice and route choice (congestion) modeling steps, also allows capturing losses induced by departure choice changes within the nested logit transport model.

The indirect costs to society due to a road closure contain actually more than the loss in CS. Additional costs of, for example, emissions and accidents, so called external costs, are not necessarily directly felt by the road users, but are induced by them and imposed on others. These additional cost categories depend, for example, on speed, distance, vehicle and road type. Specific link-based formulas incorporating the relevant influencing factors as, for example, suggested by Arbeitsgruppe Verkehrsplanung (1997) may serve as a detailed basis for calculation.

3.3.4 Demonstrating example

The following example illustrates the application of the formulas and the calculation of indirect losses (excluding external costs) with regard to a fictional network (see Figure 11). Nodes *1*, *2* and *3* represent traffic regions such as cities. The links *a*, *b*, *c* and *d* are links connecting the cities. They could stand for travel alternatives in respect of modes and routes. In accordance to the calculations made later in the Baden-Wuerttemberg case study, there are assumed to exist no alternatives in respect to mode. In the example link *a* and *c* represent roads or a sequence of road sections on different routes in both directions. The same holds for links *b* and *d*. The links are assumed to have no capacity constraints. Therefore all users would choose the route with the lowest expected cost – the lowest generalized costs – which would be links *a* and *b*.

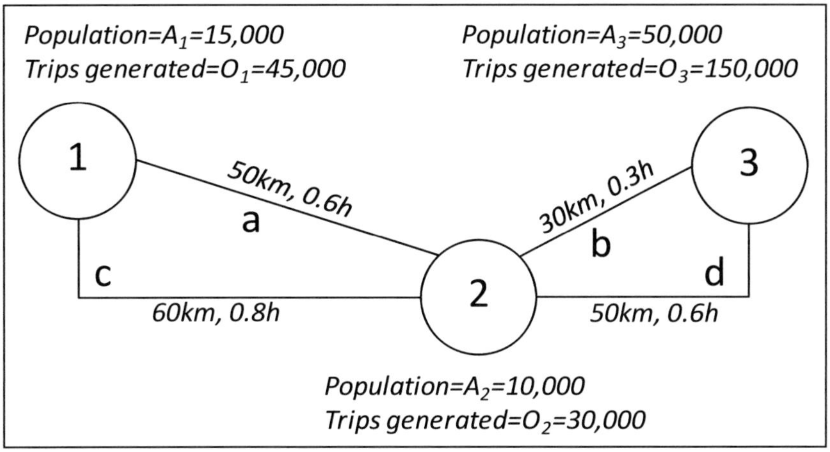

Figure 11: Exemplary network configuration

The generalized costs here comprise the sum of the monetized time and distance. The value of distance is assumed to be 0.15 Euro/km and the value of time is 5 Euro/h. Table 6 displays the calculated generalized costs in the intact network ($c_{ij\ Ref}$) and the additional cost in the event of a disruption of link *a* ($\Delta_a c_{ij}$) or link *b* ($\Delta_b c_{ij}$). Alpha is assumed to be 0.1 Euro^{-1}. The population at each node serves as an attractiveness measure. Together with the assumed number of trips generated at each node, the number of trips between the nodes (T_{ij}) is derived according to formula (3-16). The results are depicted in Table 6.

T_{ij}^{Ref}	1	2	3	$\Delta_a c_{ij}$ [EUR]	1	2	3
1	24,427	5,699	14,875	1	0	2.5	2.5
2	3,689	7,027	19,284	2	2.5	0	0
3	7,059	14,138	128,803	3	2.5	0	0
c_{ij}^{Ref} [EUR]	1	2	3	$\Delta_b c_{ij}$ [EUR]	1	2	3
1	0	10.5	17	1	0	0	4.5
2	10.5	0	6	2	0	0	4.5
3	17	6	0	3	4.5	4.5	0

Table 6: Number of trips, generalized costs in intact network and changes in generalized costs when link a or b are disrupted

The expected maximum utility ($EMU_{J|i}$) in the reference case is calculated using formula (3-17), the expected maximum utilities in the scenario cases are each approximated with formula

(3-23). The medium-term and short-term losses are derived according to formulas (3-24) and (3-25). The results are summarized in Table 7.

[EUR]	O_i^{Ref}	EMU_{JIi}^{Ref}	$EMU_{JIi}^{case\ a}$	$EMU_{JIi}^{case\ b}$	$\Delta_a CS_{JIi}$	$\Delta_b CS_{JIi}$	$(-)\Delta_a c_{ij} * T_{ij}^{Ref}$	$(-)\Delta_b c_{ij} * T_{ij}^{Ref}$
1	45,000	102.27	101.27	101.12	-45,004	-51,875	-51,433	-66,936
2	30,000	106.62	106.35	104.38	-8,069	-67,252	-9,222	-86,777
3	150,000	109.72	109.62	109.23	-15,442	-73,924	-17,648	-95,386
				Medium-term losses (sum)=	-68,515	-193,051		
						Short-term losses (sum)=	-78,303	-249,098

Table 7: Accessibility in the intact network, changes of accessibility in the disrupted network and CS

In the example, the outcome of the loss calculation of the closure of links *a* and *b* shows that the disruption of link *b* entails much larger indirect losses than a closure of link *a*, both in the medium-term (193,051 Euro versus 68,515 Euro) as well as in the short-term (249,098 Euro versus 78,303 Euro). The temporal distinctions cause a reduction in daily losses by ca. 10% for link *a* and ca. 20% for link *b*. This reduction in losses from the short- to the medium-term can be explained by changes in destination choice, and their less impacting influence on utility reduction in comparison to the disutility due to harmful route choice modifications. In this example, link *b* would be considered as being more critical than link *a* for short- term and for medium-term closures.

3.4 Multiple simultaneous failures and critical infrastructures

Having so far concentrated on single road sections' failures when it comes to calculating the indirect losses and identifying critical infrastructures, this chapter reveals interesting insights into the influence of the combination of multiple simultaneously closed road sections on indirect losses. It is possible that the combined failure of two road sections entails larger, smaller or equal indirect costs compared with the sum of their individual failure losses. This implies that the identified CIs might be more or less critical, depending on what event caused the disruption, and which other road sections are therefore simultaneously closed. In his work, Szimba (2008) explored the single and combined implementation of European transportation infrastructure projects and the corresponding benefits. He differentiates the effects on the benefits caused by the combined implementation in terms of substitutability, complementarity and additivity. His idea is here analogously applied to the removal instead of the addition of infrastructure sections and to the corresponding costs[28] instead of the benefits. In analogy to

[28] Here: negative benefits

Szimba (2008), Table 8 summarizes the utility and cost implications aligned with the substitutability, complementarity and additivity of two infrastructure sections/projects p_A and p_B.

	Utility implications	Cost implications
Complementarity	$U(p_A \cup p_B) > U(p_A) + U(p_B)$	$C(p_A \cup p_B) < C(p_A) + C(p_B)$
Substitutability	$U(p_A \cup p_B) < U(p_A) + U(p_B)$	$C(p_A \cup p_B) > C(p_A) + C(p_B)$
Additivity	$U(p_A \cup p_B) = U(p_A) + U(p_B)$	$C(p_A \cup p_B) = C(p_A) + C(p_B)$

Table 8: Complementarity, substitutability and additivity of road sections and their implications in respect of utility and costs (own illustration in analogy to Szimba (2008), p.41f)

Two road sections are complements to each other if their combined removal entails fewer costs than the sum of the costs if they fail individually. Analogously, the benefits of the two road sections realized together exceed the benefits of the sum of their individual benefit assessment. Table 9 and Figure 12 exemplify the context of complementary road sections in a fictional network. The number next to a link corresponds to the costs a user has to bear when driving on this link. All users are assumed to choose the route with the lowest overall cost to get from the Origin *O* to the Destination *D*. In this scenario the costs associated with the complete network are six cost units. If only link *A* shuts down, then the users are faced with five additional cost units. A closure of link *B* entails three additional cost units. In the event that link *A* and link *B* are interrupted simultaneously, the users' costs rise by six cost units, which is less than 5+3=8 additional cost units as sum of their individual closures. Road sections have complementary characteristics if they are on the same route between *O* and *D*. The detours associated with the individual closed links partly overlap.

Scenarios Complementarity	User cost c	$\Delta c_{ToReference}$
Reference	6	-
Link A disrupted	11	5
Link B disrupted	9	3
Link A and B disrupted	12	6
Scenarios Substitutability	**User cost c**	**$\Delta c_{ToReference}$**
Reference	5	-
Link A disrupted	8	3
Link B disrupted	5	0
Link A and B disrupted	10	5
Scenarios Additivity	**User cost c**	**$\Delta c_{ToReference}$**
Reference	5	-
Link A disrupted	6	1
Link B disrupted	6	1
Link A and B disrupted	7	2

Table 9: Example scenarios on substitutability, complementarity and additivity of road sections

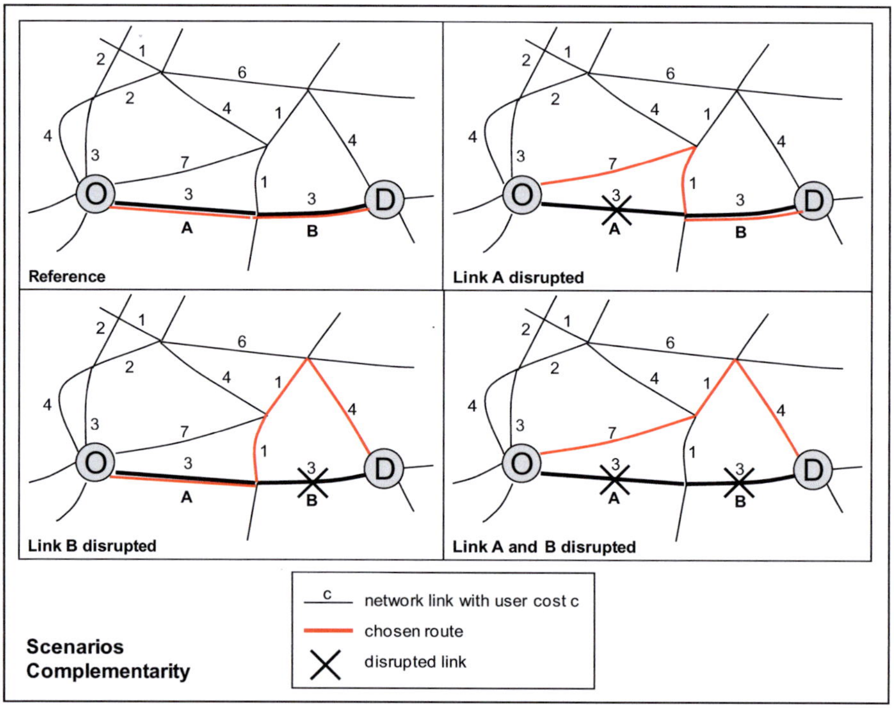

Figure 12: Example scenario on complementarity of road sections (own illustration in analogy to Szimba (2008), p.38f)

Figure 13 and Table 9 demonstrate an example of two substitute road sections. While their individual closures add three and zero units to the user costs (sum=3+0), their combined disruption costs five additional units, which is higher. Two road sections fall into this category, if they are on two different routes between *O* and *D*. If only one of the two links is closed, the other link substitutes for the closed one on the detour.

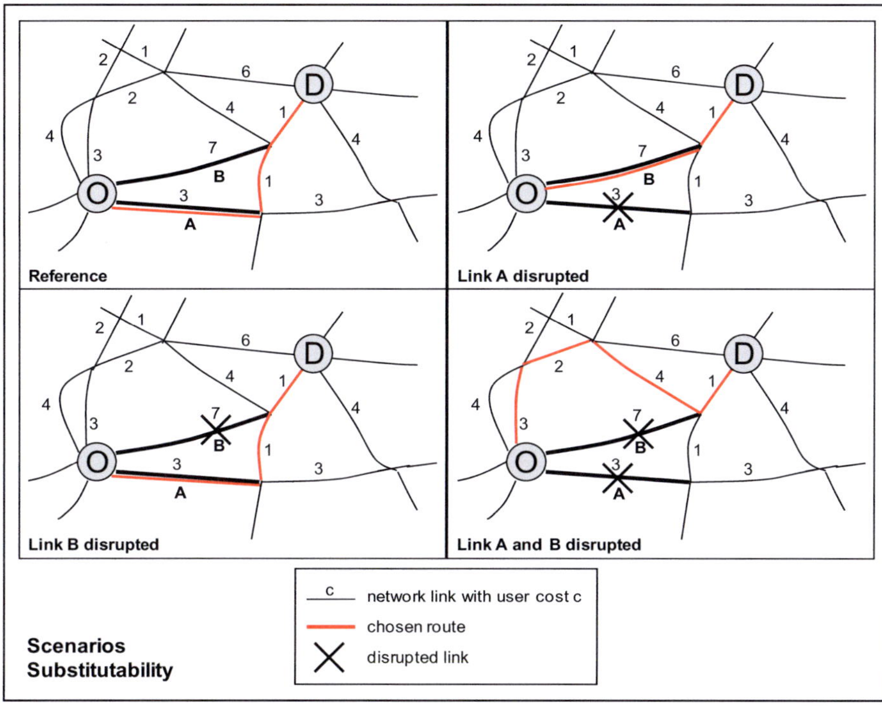

Figure 13: Example scenario on substitutability of road sections (own illustration in analogy to Szimba (2008), p.38f)

Two road sections show additive cost characteristics if their detours due to their closures do not interact. They may but do not have to lie on the same route between *O* and *D*. In this case, their individual shut downs are as costly as their combined disruption. This is exemplified in Figure 14 and Table 9.

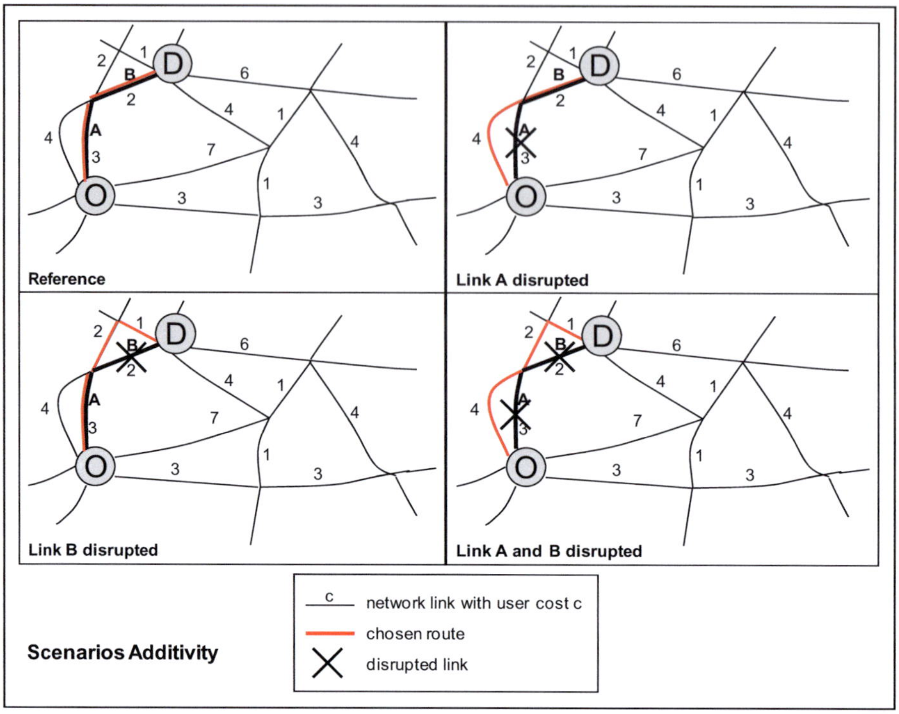

Figure 14: Example scenario on additivity of road sections (own illustration in analogy to Szimba (2008), p.38f)

Applying the common CI identification procedure by looking at the losses connected to the failure of individual infrastructures, link A is considered more critical than link B in the substitutability and complementarity scenarios. However, if they fail together, their combined criticality falls in the event of complementarity, and rises in the event of substitutability. This implies that the CI identification in networks on an individual basis only accounts for single failures. In combination with the failure of another CI, losses might be reduced or could even be amplified. Therefore a profound CI identification on a multi-hazard basis should also take into account the effects of multiple closures. This could be done on a case by case basis after the most important infrastructures have been identified on a single failure basis, and the amount of infrastructures under consideration is hence significantly reduced. In Chapter 6, two realistic multiple road failure scenarios demonstrate the application of the indirect loss calculation methodology and the implications of simultaneous multiple road failures on the identification of CIs.

3.5 Interdependencies with other infrastructures

As mentioned in the literature review, a very crucial aspect in the context of CIs is the interdependencies between different infrastructure systems. In accordance with simultaneous multiple failures of different road sections, where indirect losses are over- or underestimated depending on the combination of links within the link set, the same could be assessed in respect to (inter) dependencies between the road transportation infrastructure and other infrastructures. Complementarity, substitutability and additivity of infrastructures may exist. Focusing on road sections and their disruption, geographical and logical interdependencies appear most important.

Changes in the human decision making caused by a road infrastructure disruption, like mode or destination choice changes, could be considered as logical interdependencies. An example of a geographical interdependency is a road section passing over a railway line via a bridge. Assuming the bridge fails, e.g. as a result of an earthquake, both modes' infrastructures lose their serviceability. Assuming further that the road and railway section substitute for each other as the main connection between two cities, the effect of substitutability occurs, resulting in an underestimation of the indirect loss potential and therefore a too low criticality assessment of both infrastructures compared to their individual assessment. An example of complementarity effects may be found in an intermodal network, e.g. a road – ship – train – road transportation chain, with ship and train simultaneously affected geographically by a flood. This may result in lower costs, when circumventing both modes via road, than the sum of the modes' individual circumventions in the event of individual disruptions.

The concrete calculation of geographical interdependency effects on the criticality assessment of road sections could be done on a case by case basis, e.g. coinstantaneously with a hazard evaluation. This analysis, however, goes beyond the scope of this thesis, and therefore leaves further issues open for research.

3.6 Recapitulation of the identification of critical road infrastructures

Based on the identified research gaps, this chapter formulated the objectives of this study and set the analytical basis for their achievement. The identification of critical road infrastructures shall hence be performed by calculating the monetized (first-order) indirect losses of single and multiple road sections' failures for varying closure durations, and the results shall be set into the context of risk. The temporal distinction differentiates short-term losses comprising indirect losses due to detouring and medium-term losses, including indirect losses caused by detouring and mode/destination choice changes. The theoretical background of a nested logit model with the retrievable CS changes due to changes in travel costs provides the background for the loss calculation and criticality assessment in this study. The approximated derived measure for short- and medium-term losses spares the need of an additional complete rerun of the model, and allows a relatively easy application. Typically, criticality assessments are based on the comparison of single disruption effects. This chapter demonstrated how multiple simultaneous failures affect indirect losses, and hence also the criticality, against a background of 'realistic' failures. The implications of the interdependencies between road sections for criticality can also be transferred to the interdependencies to other types of infrastructures. However, this will not be the focus of this study.

4 Baden-Wuerttemberg case study: Approach

4.1 Overview of the methodological approach of the case study

The Baden-Wuerttemberg case study region is located in the southwest of Germany and is one of 16 Federal States ('Bundeslaender') in Germany (see Figure 15). It ranks second after Bavaria in terms of its surface area, and third after North Rhine-Westphalia and Bavaria in respect to its population. With ca. 36,000 km^2, ca. 11 million inhabitants and ca. 5 million households, its size corresponds to that of Belgium. Stuttgart is Baden-Wuerttemberg's capital, and, with its ca. 600,000 residents, forms the largest city in the state. Baden-Wuerttemberg has a relative low unemployment rate (<5%) and a relative high per capita income, and belongs therefore to one of the wealthier states in Germany (Wezel et al. (2010)). The state's supraregional road infrastructure comprises 1,552 km of motorways ('Autobahnen'), 5015 km of main roads ('Bundesstraßen'), 9,980 km of state roads ('Landesstraßen') and 12,107 km of district roads ('Kreisstraßen')[29] (Wirtschaftsministerium Baden-Württemberg (2010)). The automotive and engineering industries belong to the biggest employing sectors in the state. Compared to other states in Germany, Baden-Wuerttemberg is very prone to natural hazards, such as floods, storms and earthquakes.

Baden-Wuerttemberg was chosen for this case study due to its economic importance within Germany and in Europe, its location within Europe and therefore its supraregional relevance in terms of road transportation, its exposure to natural hazards with an associated road interruption risk, as well as the author's knowledge of the area which might be helpful in the interpretation of the results.

[29] Motorways and main roads are financed and planned by national authorities, state roads by state authorities and district roads by district authorities.

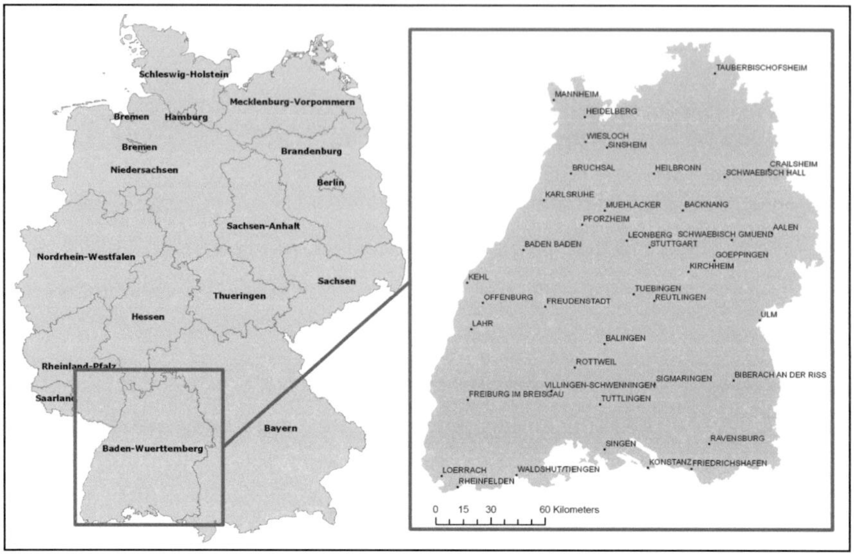

Figure 15: Germany's federal states and Baden-Wuerttemberg

Applying the loss calculation/CI identification methodology to the case study area requires the use of the following items:

a) Routable network with an assignment procedure
b) A transport model, with logit based submodels for at least one of the first three steps for the derivation of the EMU – here the destination choice
c) Tool to calculate the indirect losses and with which to derive the CI ranking

When designing a case study, various aspects have to be traded off against one another. A higher degree of accuracy with regard to one aspect often comes along with a degree of imprecision with regard to another aspect. In this case study one of the most crucial requirements is to have a detailed routable road network. A less dense network (e.g. motorways and federal roads only) would not capture all rerouting possibilities, and would therefore overestimate the short-term losses. Focusing on the area of Baden-Wuerttemberg further requires rather disaggregated traffic zones. Aggregated traffic zones with fewer traffic induction points and proportionally more intrazonal trips have a higher tendency to distort the transport model's results and the calculation of indirect losses.

For the purpose of this study an extract version of the transport model VALIDATE in the transport modeling software VISUM, a product from the PTV AG, is available and fulfills the crucial requirements concerning the network and traffic zones. It includes a dense routable road network covering Baden-Wuerttemberg, and contributes to the necessary input items a) and b). The available data/software from the transport model contains passenger car and truck **O**rigin/**D**estination (O/D)- matrices[30] for Tuesdays/Thursdays[31] as a result of the first three steps in the transport model ("Black Box" in Figure 16). Moreover, the VISUM assignment procedures with the parameters implemented in VALIDATE are available.

Coming along with the use of this extract transport model, an EMU from mode or destination choice cannot be directly retrieved from VALIDATE. Therefore separate logit models have to be estimated. For simplification, only the distribution choice step in the Black Box (here: the destination choice) is substituted by a separate logit model in order to fulfill the requirements of the loss calculation methodology. Mode choice is neglected. The self-estimated logit model pursues the goal to demonstrate the suggested loss calculation methodology in a comprehensible way, rather than displaying complicated up-to-date modeling techniques with a perfect fit to reality. The VALIDATE passenger car O/D-matrix serves for calibration purposes of the logit model, as well as VALIDATE's implemented traffic count. A tool to calculate the indirect losses (item c)) necessitates assessment parameters and a computation platform. The assessment parameters used for this study predominantly originate from the literature and statistics. Microsoft Office Excel 2007, Microsoft Visual Basic, Microsoft Office Access 2007 and MATLAB R2009b provided the software for the self implemented calculation tool. Figure 16 displays the structure of the loss calculation methodology and the connected CI identification. It also indicates that short term losses may be calculated with the help of the relevant parts in the Δ CS (**C**onsumer **S**urplus) as well as through the assessed difference of the monetized assignment results (time and distances between O/Ds in loaded network).

The following sections address all parts of the modeling process. First the details of the extracted transport model VALIDATE, with its underlying network, are introduced. Afterwards the chosen assessment parameters concerning the value of time (VOT), value of distance (VOD) and value of externalities (VOE) are presented, including a sensitivity parameter for the VOT, as results will reveal that time costs play a major role for the size of indirect losses. Subsequently the development of the logit model is described in more detail.

[30] Such an O/D matrix comprises the number of cars /trucks coming from an origin *i* (rows) going to a destination *j* (columns).

[31] Tuesdays and Thursdays are similar concerning the characteristics of daily trip volumes during a typical week.

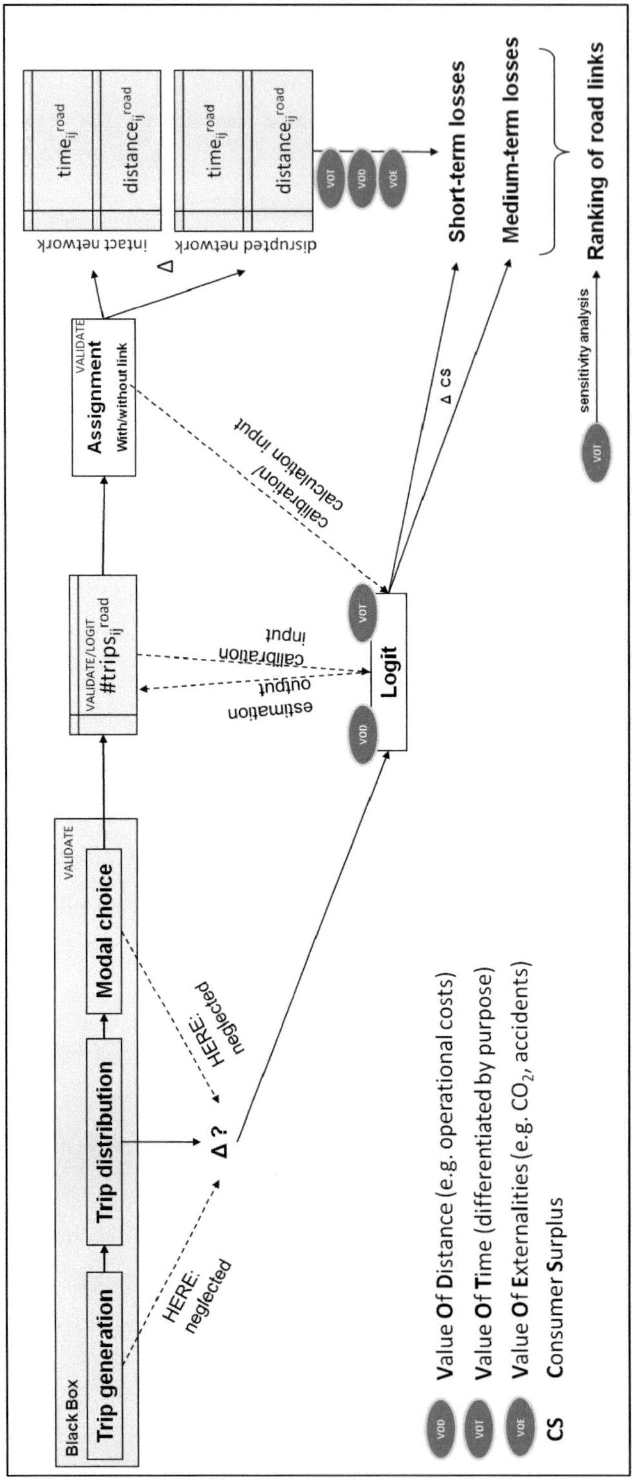

Figure 16: Overview of the modeling steps

4.2 THE TRANSPORT MODEL VALIDATE

The complete VALIDATE model implemented in the transport modeling software VISUM contains 1.6 million links and nearly 10,000 traffic zones with regard to Germany and its neighboring countries. Germany itself is represented by 9,600 traffic zones with each zone comprising ca. 8,500 inhabitants. Detailed navigation networks from NAVTEQ, a global supplier of maps, location and traffic data, constitute the underlying network model. The trip generation, distribution and modal choice for passenger transport demand is performed with VISEVA[32]. The trip generation differentiates between purpose-dependent activities (e.g. home-work, leisure-leisure, work-home), and is based on the categorization of households and persons. Trip distribution and modal choice are performed in a combined discrete choice model with three-dimensional utility matrices (origin, destination, mode) (Lohse (2004)). Commercial traffic is estimated separately by TCI Röhling, based on an approach similar to the four step modeling technique and various statistical data like distance distribution, different types of goods, import/export freight flows, etc. The assignment of the truck OD matrix is carried out together with the passenger car OD matrix in VALIDATE.

The extract version of VALIDATE available here contains 1,100 traffic zones with 270 cordon zones and 830 'real' traffic zones for the area of Baden-Wuerttemberg, and is implemented in VISUM 11.0. Cordon zones represent external origins and destinations at the boundaries of Baden-Wuerttemberg. The traffic demand has been calibrated by traffic count data from 2005/2006 provided by the German Federal Highway Research Institute. 159 traffic count sites with truck and passenger car numbers are included in this extract version of VALIDATE. The passenger car matrix comprises 16,675,555 passenger car trips and the truck matrix 534,477 truck trips. There is no differentiation by purpose. The underlying NAVTEQ network (state of 4th quarter of 2008) for the area of Baden-Wuerttemberg contains 191,362 links. VALIDATE's preset assignment procedure follows the principles of the user equilibrium with a preceding successive assignment in 5 steps (30%, 20%, 20%, 20%, 10%) to derive an initial solution from which the equilibrium is approximated. The assignment is calibrated to fit average daily traffic values on Tuesdays or Thursdays. Hourly traffic situations cannot be extracted using the applied assignment procedure. Dynamic assignment procedures in VISUM could remedy this shortcoming, but would also entail larger computation times and exceed the requirements for the purpose of this study. Since it turned out that a mere successive assignment procedure entails traffic assignment results of a similar quality with signifi-

[32] For a detailed description of the theoretical background see Lohse et al. (1997).

cantly less computation time (ca. 1.5 min) than the preset equilibrium assignment (ca. 15 min), the study uses a four step successive assignment procedure (50%, 25%, 13%, 12%) instead. The iteration volumes are based on the settings in the transport model VACLAV from the Institute for Economic Policy Research at the Karlsruhe Institute of Technology[33]. VACLAV, with its iterative assignment procedure, has successfully been applied in European projects such as TEN-STAC (NEA et al. (2004)) and the TINA-Turkey (TINA et al. (2007)). 296 one-way motorway sections between two exits pose the basis for the identification of critical road infrastructures. Each section is represented by one specific link in one direction. All other links within one section obtain the same indirect loss values as their representative link. Overall, 4,142 motorway links are considered. Some links close to the border of Baden-Wuerttemberg have been neglected to avoid distorted results due to the cut network.

4.3 The relevant assessment parameters

The assessment parameters relevant for the logit model and the monetization of the short- and medium term losses are based on the parameters predominantly used in cost-benefit assessment schemes. These parameters include time, operational cost, safety and environmental cost savings/losses. The logit model includes time and operational costs in the utility function, respectively the generalized cost function (the sum of the monetized time- and distance-based cost). Safety and environmental costs are assumed to be not directly incorporated into the road users' decision rationale, and are externally added to the losses. A consistent valuation of the components in demand estimation and assessment is pursued wherever applicable, an approach which has been recommended in the European cost-benefit scheme guidelines (TRT and CSIL (2008), p.76).

As assessment parameters, especially the valuation of travel time, are often the focus of discussion and criticism while highly determining the final results, this study abstains from trying to find the 'perfect' assessment parameters. It rather resorts to the application of readily available and widely recognized parameters. A transparent derivation of the parameters shall allow the interpretation of the results against a clear assessment background.

Where possible, an alignment with the German cost-benefit scheme in the German National Transport Infrastructure Plan is strived for. This allows communicating the results based on the assessment parameters common and more or less acknowledged by politicians, transport researchers and planners.

[33] For a detailed description of the model see Schoch (2004), p.31ff.

The following sections explain the derivation of the assessment parameters and what they comprise.

4.3.1 *The generalized costs: Value of time*

The value of time (VOT), also referred to as the value of travel-time savings (VTTS), denotes "the monetary rate at which a given travel-time saving or loss in a particular context can be compensated for by a corresponding loss or saving of money" (Gunn (2008), p.503). The VOT does herein not serve as an "input to travel decisions" but is rather the behavioral output of more complex decisions (ibid., p.508)[34]. Typically, the VOT is derived from revealed or stated preference surveys, in which historic or imaginary decisions with different settings of time and cost are recorded. Factor-cost methods (estimating the cost of all input factors saved/lost) further serve for the assessment of the VOT of freight trips (de Jong (2008)). Lacking the resources to set up surveys for all kind of situations necessitating a monetary assessment of travel-time savings or losses, national cost-benefit-schemes usually hold simple reference assessment parameter values for the VOT which are universally applicable for transportation projects in the relevant countries.

Many surveys have found that the passengers' VOT varies according to purpose, mode, sign and size of time changes, income, journey length and retirement status of travelers (Mackie et al. (2003)). While the explicit distinction by mode and purpose is prevalent in most European cost-benefit schemes, further differentiation is usually restricted to the length of the journey and the size of time changes. Income effects are usually implicitly included in the VOT as it is often expressed as fraction of the average national income per person.

Most national cost-benefit schemes used in European countries, including the one in Germany, refer to a VOT applicable to losses and benefits (Odgaard et al. (2005)). The applied VOT here aligns with these schemes. However, some studies proclaim a higher valuation of travel time losses than travel time savings (Gunn (2001); AMR and HCG (1996) cited in Wardman (1998)). Recapitulating and analyzing the AMR and HCG (1996) study in more detail, Bates and Whelan (2001) did not find any significant evidence of time gains being less valued than losses. The difference in the valuation is usually explained by the survey design or by a loss

[34] As the logit model here applied includes time-cost trading decisions in a behavioral model, it is principally possible to derive the VOT directly from the model through a regression analysis. However, since the derivation of time-cost tradeoffs is not the focus of this study and the input data (travel decisions) is itself output from another model (black-box), here readily available, justifiable values of time serve as input. Gunn (2008), p.508, principally supports this argumentation. Furthermore the outcome of the logit model would most likely lead to functions of values of time – not necessarily justifiable with empirical findings.

aversive valuation of the survey respondents (van de Kaa (2010)).

Like in Germany, many other European countries differentiate their VOT between passenger trip purposes in terms of being non-business or business. Some also distinguish non-business trips between commuting and leisure (Odgaard et al. (2005), p.37f). In the German cost-benefit scheme it is assumed (based on microeconomic surveys) that people value leisure time at a magnitude of 50% of working time. Supposing that unemployed people have a VOT of zero, and taking into account the ratio of unemployed to employed people, car passengers on a non-business trip have a VOT corresponding to ca. 20% of the average gross income of an employed person (Hogrebe et al. (1986)). The German VOT in the cost-benefit scheme was compared with the results of a Dutch willingness-to-pay survey, and proved to be of the same order (Willeke and Paulußen (1991), p.153).

The German cost-benefit scheme further assumes that travel time savings or losses for non-business passenger trips are not felt if they are smaller than a certain threshold. It uses a discounted unit value approach for non-business trips (including commuting) to account for a reduced valuation of smaller time changes. The 'actual' VOT of 6.04 Euro/person hour[35] is discounted by 30%, to 4.23 Euro/person hour, and then applied to all sizes of time changes (Willeke and Paulußen (1991) and Planco Consulting GmbH (2000) (see Figure 17).

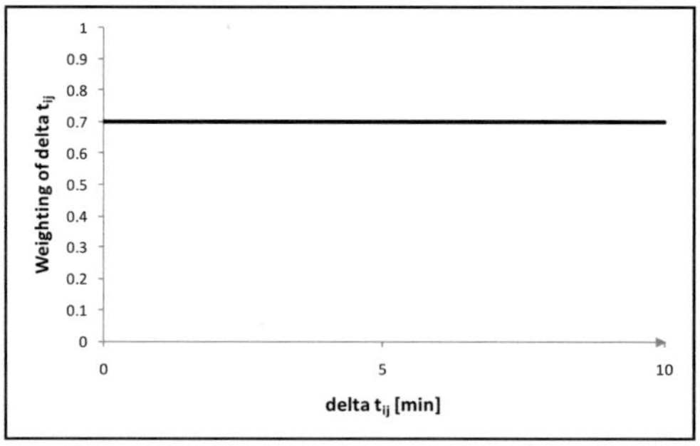

Figure 17: Discounted VOT in the German Cost-Benefit scheme in the National Transport Infrastructure Plan

Taking a reduced average VOT (RAV) tends to underestimate the valuation of larger travel time changes, and to overestimate small travel time changes. On average this does not matter, but in the event of prevailing short/long travel time changes, this approach over-

[35] Converted into 2005 prices

/underestimates benefits or losses. As the standard approach in the German cost-benefit scheme, this methodology is initially adopted for the VOT used in this study.

In the updating process of the German National Transport Infrastructure Plan and its corresponding cost-benefit time valuation scheme, the shortcomings of the RAV just mentioned are mitigated by giving the VOT a functional form. Small time changes of up to 5 minutes are suggested to be continuously discounted, while larger time changes receive the full VOT (BVU et al. (2009), p.100). This results in the following valuation (see also Figure 18):

$$time\ cost_{old} = \Delta\, t_{ij} \cdot VOT \tag{4-1}$$

$$time\ cost_{new} = f(\Delta\, t_{ij}) \cdot VOT \tag{4-2}$$

$$f(\Delta\, t_{ij}) = \begin{cases} \frac{1}{5} \cdot \Delta\, t_{ij} & \forall\, \Delta\, t_{ij} < 5 \\ \Delta\, t_{ij} & \forall\, \Delta\, t_{ij} \geq 5 \end{cases} \tag{4-3}$$

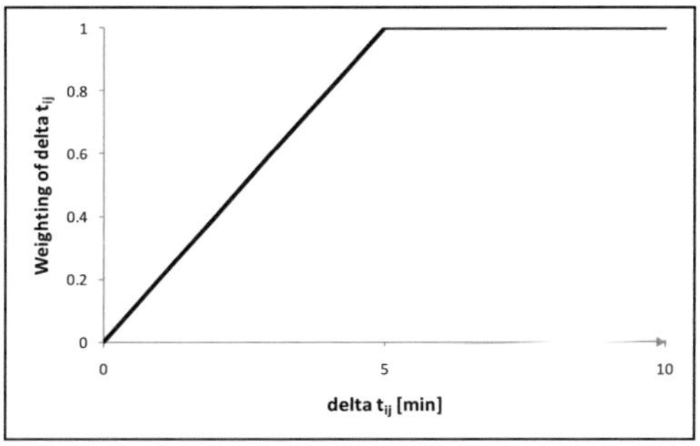

Figure 18: Standardized weighting function for small travel time differences in the updated cost-benefit scheme of the German National Transport Infrastructure Plan

For the purposes of this study, the sensitivity of the identified critical road sections to the 'new' VOT[36] evaluation scheme is analyzed, so that sections having excellent alternative routes (with less than a 5 minute detour on average) become less critical than before. For the indirect loss calculation this would entail smaller indirect losses related to short detours taking less than 5 minutes, and higher losses for longer detours. When incorporated into the logit model for destination choice, it would raise the generalized costs between all regions (all regions are more than 5 minutes away from each other) and it would also weigh time costs more strongly compared to operational (distance-based) costs in the generalized cost function. Con-

[36] The 'new' VOT is later called VOTnew in comparison to VOTold which refers to the VOT in the 'old' German National Transport Infrastructure Plan.

sequently, the logit model, and respectively the parameters of the logit model, would require a new estimation and calibration. The functional form of the VOT would entail rather complex calculations. Here, the OD matrix is assumed to stay unchanged by the VOT variation. Hence, only short-term losses are exposed to the sensitivity analysis with the new VOT.

The VOT of passengers on a business trip comprise the average gross income per employed person (22.03 Euro/person hour) and additionally weighted time dependent material costs (1.36 Euro/person hour[37]) (Birn et al. (2005)). The latter accounts for additional/ omitted transportation capacities available for other requests in the event of of travel time savings/ losses (Hogrebe et al. (1986), p.33). For freight, the VOT also comprises weighted wages (25.99 Euro/truck hour) and time dependent material costs (3.04 Euro/truck hour) (Birn et al. (2005)). The weighting is based on the vehicle type share on Baden-Wuerttemberg's roads (Statistisches Landesamt Baden-Württemberg (2010)).

Table 10 summarizes the VOT parameters[38] for the relevant purposes of this study. 'Old' refers to the RAV methodology for discounting small travel time changes for non-business trips including commuting in the German National Transport Infrastructure Plan from 2003, while 'new' refers to the updated methodology serving as sensitivity parameter for short-term loss assessment.

purpose	VOT	unit
business	23.39	Euro/person hour
non-business$_{old}$	4.23	Euro/person hour
commuting$_{old}$	4.23	Euro/person hour
non-business$_{new}$	0.00-6.04	Euro/person hour
commuting$_{new}$	0.00-6.04	Euro/person hour
freight	29.04	Euro/truck hour

Table 10: Overview of the VOT by trip purpose used for this study

[37] [Euro/passenger car hour] was transferred into [Euro/person hour] by division by the occupancy rate (OR).
[38] Converted into 2005 prices

4.3.2 The generalized costs: Value of distance

The value of distance (VOD) consists of the operating costs (excluding fuel) and the average costs for gasoline/diesel (excluding value added tax (VAT)). The operating costs are derived from German National Transport Infrastructure Plan (Birn et al. (2005), p.167) weighted by the transport performance share on each road type in Baden-Wuerttemberg in 2005 (Statistisches Landesamt Baden-Württemberg (2010)) and by the share of diesel and gasoline in passenger cars (Birn et al. (2005), p.163), and the share of truck type for the VOD for freight (Statistisches Landesamt Baden-Württemberg (2010)). In 2005 values, this results in 11.33 cent/passenger car km and 22.12 cent/truck km. The average fuel costs for passenger cars (AFC_{pc}) contain an assumed average consumption of 7.5 liter/100 km[39] multiplied by the fuel type weighted (Birn et al. (2005), p.163) average gasoline/diesel prices (excluding 16% VAT) at filling stations in 2005 (Eurostat (2010)). The average fuel costs for trucks (AFC_{trucks}) assume an average consumption of 20 liter/100 km[40] multiplied, as well, by the average diesel prices (excluding 16% VAT) at filling stations in 2005. The petroleum tax (65.45 cent per liter), mainly imposed to account for road infrastructure maintenance and re-investments as well as environmental externalities, is included in the prices. For simplification purposes, the fuel consumption here is only distance- and not speed-dependent and road charges for heavy duty vehicles are neglected.

$$AFC_{pc} = \left(1.06 \frac{€}{gasoline \times l} \times 0.828 \frac{gasoline}{passenger\ car} + 0.92 \frac{€}{diesel \times l} \times 0.172 \frac{diesel}{passenger\ car}\right) \times 7.5 \frac{l}{100km} = 0.0775\ \frac{€}{km} \quad (4\text{-}4)$$

$$AFC_{trucks} = \left(0.92 \frac{€}{diesel \times l}\right) \times 20 \frac{l}{100km} = 0.1840\ \frac{€}{km} \quad (4\text{-}5)$$

The operating and fuel costs add up to ca. 19 cent/pc km and ca. 41 cent/truck km (see also Table 11).

A reasonable assumption is that the VOD per person is the VOD divided by the occupancy rate, implying that operating costs are shared by all car occupants. The occupancy rate (OR), differentiated by purpose, is derived from the German mobility study (infas and DIW (2003)) as it allows a more detailed differentiation by purpose as required here. Two tables are of rel-

[39] Assumption based on Deutsches Institut für Wirtschaftsforschung (2010) and discounted to 7.5 l/100km because of the focus on motorway instead of city traffic with the latter's stop-and-go traffic.
[40] Assumption based on Birn et al. (2005), p.168

evance: the number of trips per person per purpose per weekday as a car driver (*cd*) and as a car passenger (*cp*)[41]. The OR is then calculated for each purpose in the following way:

$$occupancy\ rate = \frac{1+\frac{\#\ of\ trips\ per\ cp\ on\ Tuesdays}{\#\ of\ trips\ per\ cd\ on\ Tuesdays}+1+\frac{\#\ of\ trips\ per\ cp\ on\ Thursdays}{\#\ of\ trips\ per\ cd\ on\ Thursdays}}{2} \quad (4\text{-}6)$$

The resulting ORs and the adjusted VOD parameters are summarized in Table 11.

purpose	OR	VOD	unit
passenger cars		0.1908	Euro/pc km
business	1.02	0.1871	Euro/person km
non-business	1.46	0.1307	Euro/person km
commuting	1.24	0.1539	Euro/person km
freight		0.4051	Euro/truck km

Table 11: Overview of the OR and VOD by trip purpose used for this study

4.3.3 *Value of Externalities*

Time and operational costs are both borne by the transport users themselves, and are therefore taken into account in their transport decisions. But there are more costs to society, the so called external costs, which are not directly considered by transport users unless they are incorporated in, for example, infrastructure charging schemes (which is not the case so far). Undisputably environmental costs like air pollution, climate change and noise fall into this category (Maibach et al. (2008)). Accident costs are only external as far as they exceed the collective and own risk anticipation and they are not covered by insurance (ibid., p.14).

VISUM offers an automatic tool for external cost calculation. However, this was not available for this study. Introducing a self-made profound link-based external cost calculation module in the OD based indirect loss calculation of this study would significantly raise the computation time and require large efforts. Simplifying the calculation technique, for example by making emissions only dependent on distance and/or average speed, neglects the crucial connection to individual driving speeds on various network links during different times of the day. The transport and loss calculation model used shows results averaged over a day, but does not focus on individual hours, which would be necessary for a more detailed analysis. Calculations with only distance-dependent external costs showed a distortion of the results

[41] Business trips contain 'business trips' only, commuting trips comprise the weighted average of trips to 'education' and 'work', while non-business trips include the weighted average of 'shopping', 'leisure', 'accompany' and 'private errands'. The weighting is undertaken based on the percentage of trips of car drivers by each purpose category as an average of Tuesdays and Thursdays.

that could not easily be justified. In this case, the ratio between regional emissions plus safety costs and operational plus time costs is only about 0.5% (median) considering all links (see Figure 19). Thinking in reverse - adding a link instead of deleting one - this would mean, that environmental and safety costs could be neglected in the official cost benefit analysis in the German National Transport Plan ('Bundesverkehrswegeplan') as they would hardly contribute to the overall costs/benefits compared to the operational and time cost/benefit components.

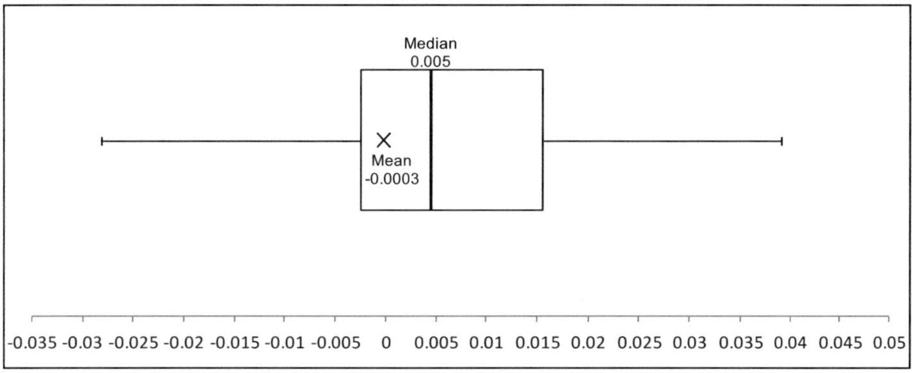

Figure 19: Box-Whisker-Plot of the ratio between regional emissions plus safety costs and operational plus time costs calculated in the indirect cost model with simplified assumptions

For the purpose of this study an anonymous, confidential table with cost-benefit data of all road projects (281 motorway projects, 1,872 main road projects) in the German National Transport Plan is available. The analysis of the data shows that additional costs (environmental and accident costs) pose a surcharge of ca. 25% on operating and time costs (on the basis of the median) (BMVBS (2010b)). Figure 20 and Figure 21 display Box-Whisker-Plots of the ratio between emissions plus safety savings and operational plus time cost savings of German motorway and main road projects in the National Transport Plan[42]. The outliers are defined according to Tukey (1977) as the data greater than 1.5 times the difference between the 3rd and 1st quartiles (IQR) from the 3rd and 1st quartiles respectively. Accordingly, the data contains 8% outliers based on motorway projects and 7% based on main road projects. The plots show that the outliers highly influence the average value in comparison to the median.

[42] The relevant categories in the National Transport Plan correspond to the classes here applied in the following way: NE=time cost savings; NB2a+NB2b=operational cost savings; NS=safety savings; NU2a+NU2d=regional emission cost savings.

In order to give consideration to the external costs in a justifiable and easy understandable way, for the purpose of the indirect cost calculation in this study, the average median value of ca. 25% serves as fixed markup on individual costs (operating and time costs), representing the value of externalities (VOE).

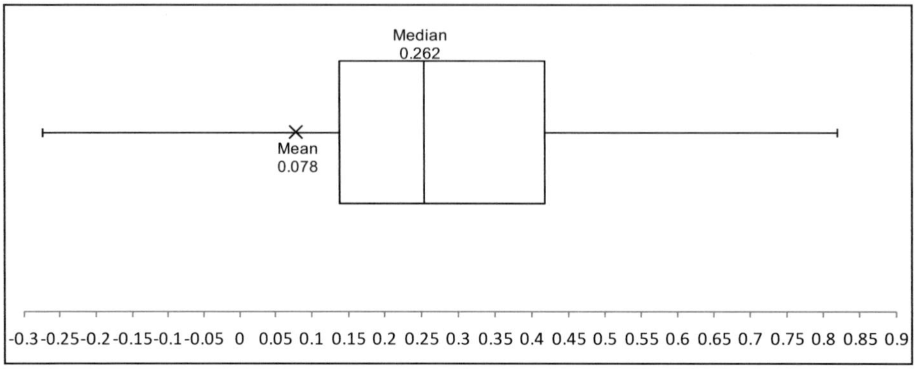

Figure 20: Box-Whisker-Plot of the relation between regional emissions and safety savings to operational and time savings of German motorway Projects in the National transport plan

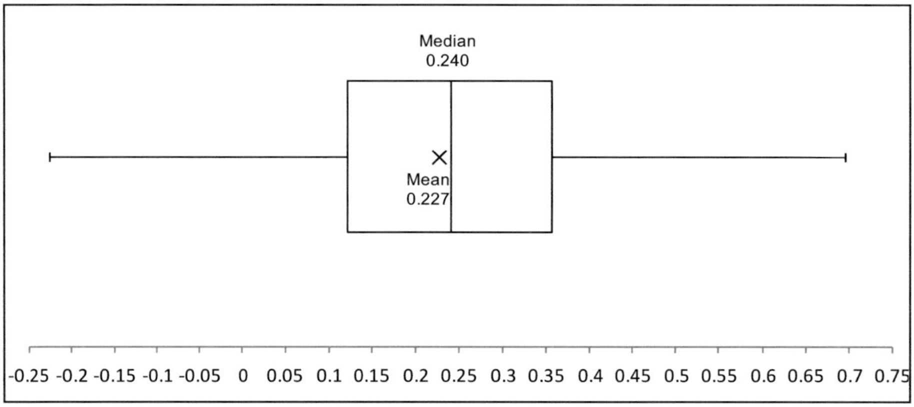

Figure 21: Box-Whisker-Plot of the relation between regional emissions and safety savings to operational and time savings of German main road projects in the National Transport Plan

In contrast to the calculation of indirect losses due to road disruption, the National Transport Plan evaluates the indirect benefits of additional road capacity. It is assumed that considering a benefit or cost calculation, the relations of the cost categories to each other are comparable. Moreover, additional road capacity in the National Transport Plan means, depending on the specific project, either the upgrade of an existing road section by increasing the number of lanes or the construction of new road sections. Although, new road sections better reflect the reverse of completely closed road sections than additional road lanes, an extraction of the more relevant road projects is not possible, since the projects' cost benefit data is only available in an anonymous form.

4.4 ESTIMATION OF THE LOGIT MODEL

As mentioned in section 3.2, trip destination changes are most likely to happen for private trips, and therefore the medium-term loss modeling with the estimated logit model concentrates on this purpose. The available VALIDATE freight matrix (number of trucks per OD), as well as the passenger car trip matrices for the other purposes of business and commuting, contribute as an external input to the assignment process to integrate their share of traffic.

4.4.1 PREPARATION OF THE AVAILABLE MATRICES FOR THE PURPOSE OF THE STUDY

The available VALIDATE passenger car matrix serves as the major input in the estimation of the passenger logit model. However, it first requires some transformations in order to establish adequate interfaces, and to benefit from them in the calibration process. In this context two preliminary steps need to be undertaken (see Figure 22) before the actual estimation process can be initialized (see Figure 24).

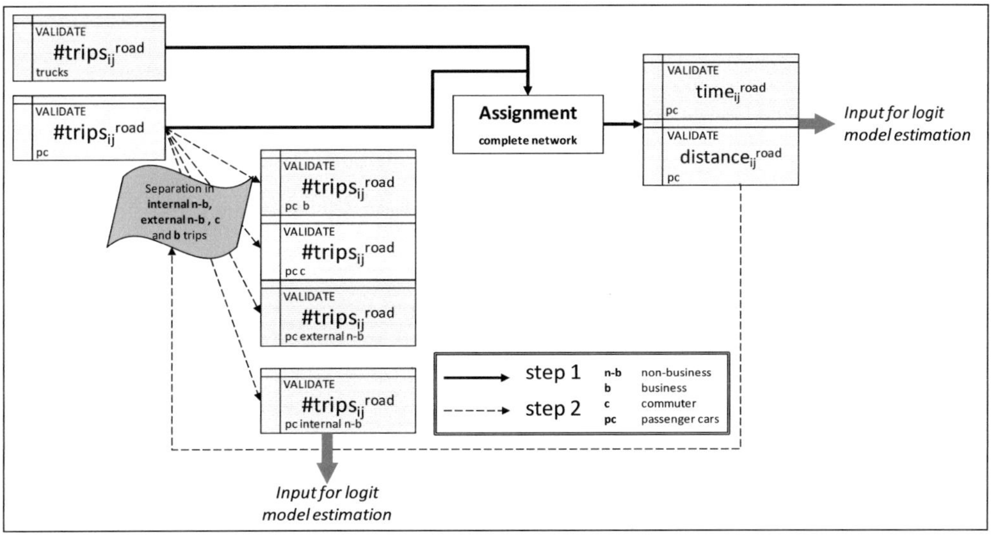

Figure 22: Preliminary steps in the estimation of the logit model

STEP 1: ASSIGNMENT OF THE VALIDATE MATRICES AND CALCULATION OF PERFORMANCE INDICATORS

In this initial step, the available VALIDATE OD matrices for passenger cars (pc) and trucks are fed into the assignment procedure, thereby providing the average distance and duration between ODs in the loaded network.

STEP 2: SEPARATION OF THE VALIDATE MATRIX INTO INTERNAL/EXTERNAL NON-BUSINESS (N-B), BUSINESS (B) AND COMMUTER TRIPS (C)

The VALIDATE passenger car trip OD matrix contains internal and external trips in Baden-Wuerttemberg (Figure 23). Internal trips start and end inside Baden-Wuerttemberg, external trips start and/or end outside Baden-Wuerttemberg. As mentioned in Chapter 4.2, external origins and destinations are represented as cordon zones at the boundaries of Baden-Wuerttemberg. The actual length and origins/destinations of trips are therefore unknown. This spoils their adequacy as input for the logit model. Thus they are further treated only as external input in the assignment process. In this context, the original VALIDATE passenger car OD matrix first needs to be separated into an internal and external trip matrix according to the locations of the origins and the destinations.

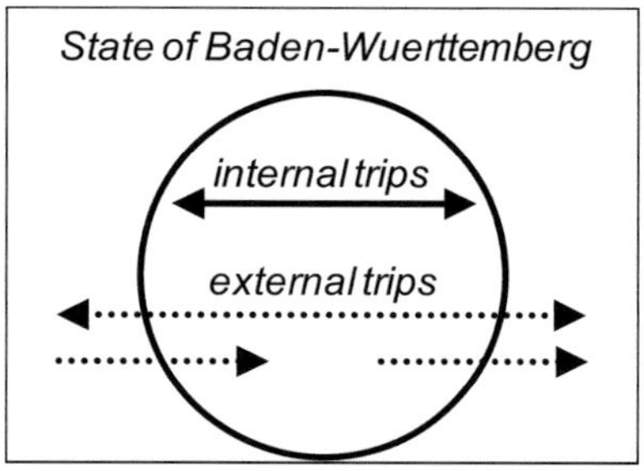

Figure 23: Distinction between internal and external trips

The original VALIDATE passenger car trip matrix is the product of the trip generation, distribution and mode choice. Although VALIDATE's trip generation purposes include among others 'home-work', 'work-work' and 'work-home', this information is not automatically passed on to the last modeling step. The available matrix thus lacks information on purposes. The differentiation by purposes is, however, crucial in assessing the indirect losses as the result of a road closure. A simple approximation of a 'real' trip's purpose is therefore undertaken by separating the passenger car trip matrix into 'business' (on duty), 'commuting' and 'non-business' (private trips like shopping or leisure) matrices.

The share of purposes in trips is derived from the German mobility study (infas and DIW (2003)) by averaging the tables representing trips according to distance classes and trip purposes for Tuesdays and Thursdays[43]. One drawback comes with this procedure: the tables in the mobility study relate to trips per person, while the PTV matrix relates to trips per car. The multiplication with the occupancy rate could remedy this problem. However, the occupancy rate is again dependent on the trip purpose which is not available at this time. There are other tables foregoing this specific problem, e.g. trips per purpose and distance class per car driver. Yet, this table neglects the distinct purpose weighting on different weekdays, though it makes, for example, a great difference in the number of business trips, if a work day is taken as a reference, or if it is averaged over the whole week including the weekend. There is a shortcoming, no matter which table is chosen. The applied procedure seems to be the most appropriate accepting the deficiency that accompanies it.

After extracting the purposes' share in trips from the German mobility study (infas and DIW (2003)) all passenger car trips in the original VALIDATE matrix are classified into the three purposes according to their OD travel distance category. Again there is one drawback. The trip length is not the actual length between ODs, but only the length to the cordon zone. This partly results in an over- and underestimation of business and non-business trips within distance classes.

4.4.2 THE ESTIMATION OF THE LOGIT MODEL FOR NON-BUSINESS PURPOSES

The goal of setting up the logit model is to be able to demonstrate the indirect loss calculation methodology and to identify critical infrastructures within a 'real' network. Some simplifying assumptions counteract data restrictions and help to meet the required conformity with VALIDATE. For example, the VOT and VOD are assumed to be fixed inputs as explained in the description of the assessment parameters. Figure 24 gives an overview of the estimation procedure of the logit model, with more detailed explanations concerning the various elements in the following paragraphs. The model is based on the formulas as explained in section 3.3.3.

[43] The available VALIDATE matrix represents Tuesdays and Thursdays.

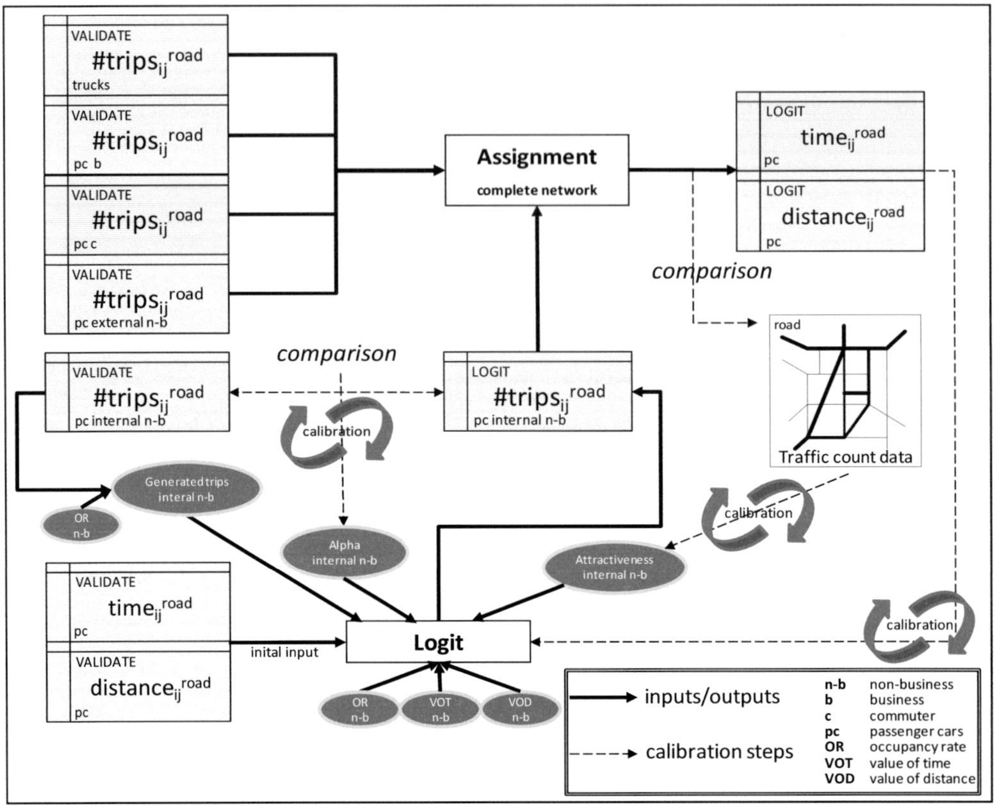

Figure 24: Estimation process of the logit model

The initial fixed and variable (subject to calibration) inputs to the model are:

a) The generated internal non-business trips as fixed input

b) The performance matrices of duration and distances for passenger cars as a result of the assignment, initially retrieved from the original assignment with the VALIDATE matrices for freight and passenger cars as variable input

c) The non-business trips' value of time (VOT) as well as value of distance (VOD) to calculate the generalized costs as fixed input

d) An initial attractiveness value for each region as variable input

e) An initial alpha value for internal non-business trips as variable input

The logit model with initial parameters calculates a passenger non-business internal trip matrix which is divided by the occupancy rate (OR) to retrieve the number of passenger cars (pc)

for non-business internal trips. Distance distributions and a comparison of the attracted trips of a region in the adjusted VALIDATE matrix serve for calibration purposes. After adding up all passenger car matrices (internal/external/business/non-business/commuter), the two vehicle matrices (passenger cars and trucks) are then assigned to the network. New duration and distance performance matrices come along with it, as well as a traffic-count-fit-analysis to further calibrate the logit model. The following paragraphs explain the various input parameters and their calibration in more detail.

THE GENERATED TRIPS IN A REGION

Usually the mode choice succeeds the trip distribution step. Here, the mode choice is neglected, and only passenger car trips are considered. The outcome of the trip distribution is person-based (one trip equals one person travelling) and not car-based (one car travelling) like in the available VALIDATE matrices. Therefore the internal non-business (n-b) passenger car (pc) trip matrix converted from the original VALIDATE matrix is multiplied by an occupancy rate (OR). This serves as input for the generated trips per region by summing up all trips originating in one region.

ATTRACTIVENESS CALCULATION

A destination's attractiveness is an indicator on how attractive a region is in respect to performing certain activities. Here, non-business trips are assumed to be attracted by the population and the number of social insurance contributing work places in this region (Statistische Landesämter (2007)). The standardized statistical values of work places and population are weighted according to the percentage of shopping trips (29%) to other non-business trips (71%) on Tuesdays and Thursdays (infas and DIW (2003)).

The regionalization in VALIDATE differs in terms of the statistical regions. Where possible, the data is matched with the region's name. Bigger cities, like Stuttgart, belong to one statistical region, but correspond to many regions in VALIDATE. In this case, the number of inhabitants in different parts of the city, published by the cities themselves, fills the gaps[44]. Where this is not possible, the statistical data of a region is divided into the corresponding traffic zones following a weighting given by the city type classification in VALIDATE.

Other combinations like 100% population as a single attracting factor or a combination with commuter statistics, as well as an easier statistical region matching, did not deliver as satisfying results in the traffic count fit, the trip length distribution and the number of attracted trips

[44] Retrieved from the cities' homepages, where available, for the year 2005, otherwise 2008 or 2009

in comparison to the adjusted reference VALIDATE pc matrix.

ALPHA ESTIMATION AND CALIBRATION

The estimation of the alpha parameter and the calculation of the corresponding trip matrices are performed in the software MATLAB. The number of trips generated in a region, the OR, the generalized costs (including the VOT, VOD and initial VALIDATE duration and distance matrices) and an initial attractiveness value are considered as constant.

Alpha's calibration process follows a straightforward approach. For each alpha ranging between 0.000 and 1.000, the corresponding trip probability is calculated and compared with the trip probability in the according adjusted reference VALIDATE matrix. This comparison follows three different principles. The first minimizes the sum of the average absolute difference between the probabilities for trip ends in the estimated matrix and in the VALIDATE matrix over all trip generating regions, resulting in the mean relative error (mre) (based on PTV AG (2009), p.390):

$$mre = \sum_I \frac{\sum_J \left|T_{ij} - T_{ij}^{est}\right|}{T_i} = \sum_I \sum_J \left|p_{ij}^{est} - p_{ij}\right| \tag{4-7}$$

I= index of Origins

J= index of Destinations

T_i= *number of trips generated in region i*

T_{ij}= *number of trips going from i to j according to the VALIDATE matrix*

T_{ij}^{est}=*number of estimated trips going from i to j*

p_{ij}= *probability for a trip going from i to j according to the VALIDATE matrix*

p_{ij}^{est}= *estimated probability for a trip going from i to j*

The second is a modified version of the minimized mre. Here the estimated number of trips serves as relative value in the dominator instead of the number of trips within a region. The mean relative error modified (mrem) is calculated as follows:

$$mrem = \sum_I \sum_J \frac{\left|T_{ij}^{est} - T_{ij}\right|}{T_{ij}^{est}} = \sum_I \sum_J \frac{\left|p_{ij}^{est} - p_{ij}\right|}{p_{ij}^{est}} \tag{4-8}$$

The second one maximizes the coefficient of determination ($R^2 \in [0,1]$) as an indicator of how well the estimated and the VALIDATE matrix values correlate.

$$R^2 = \left(\frac{\sum_I \sum_J (p_{ij} - \bar{p})(p_{ij}^{est} - \overline{p^{est}})}{\sqrt{\sum_I \sum_J (p_{ij} - \bar{p})^2 \sum_I \sum_J (p_{ij}^{est} - \overline{p^{est}})^2}} \right)^2 \tag{4-9}$$

p_{ij}= *probability for a trip going from i to j according to the VALIDATE matrix*

$\bar{p}$=*mean probability in VALIDATE matrix*

p_{ij}^{est}= *estimated probability for a trip going from i to j*

$\overline{p^{est}}$=*mean estimated probability*

The optimal alphas with the corresponding trip probability matrices are multiplied with the generated trips to obtain a passenger OD matrix which is then compared to the trip length distribution of the original adjusted VALIDATE matrix. It turns out that this estimation procedure entails an extreme underestimation of short- (with mrem) or long-distance trips (with the mre and R2), with respectively too low alphas (<0.2) or too high alphas (>0.9). Changes in the attractiveness parameter did not significantly improve the results. A different approach was therefore tested and proved to be successful.

Therein a reference alpha parameter is estimated based on the adjusted non-business, internal pc VALIDATE reference matrix. This is done by deriving an average generalized cost value for an average trip in the matrix. Trips of length zero, representing trips within a traffic zone, are set to 0.1 km, as they would otherwise not be taken into account when calculating the average trip length. The average trip length of ca. 8.5 km is then multiplied with the non-business VOD of 0.1307 Euro/km, and added to the product of the average distance and the VOT of 4.23 Euro/h divided by an assumed average speed of 75 km/h. The reciprocal of the average generalized costs is 0.632 and is further used as reference alpha. The distance distribution with an assumption of 65 km/h or 85 km/h, leading to alphas of 0.60 and 0.65 respectively, did not show as satisfying results as with an assumption of 75 km/h. As Figure 25 shows, an alpha of 0.60 underestimates the number of short-distance trips, but has a better fit in the long-distance trip distribution. The reverse holds for an alpha of 0.65, while an alpha of 0.632 is in the middle of the two.

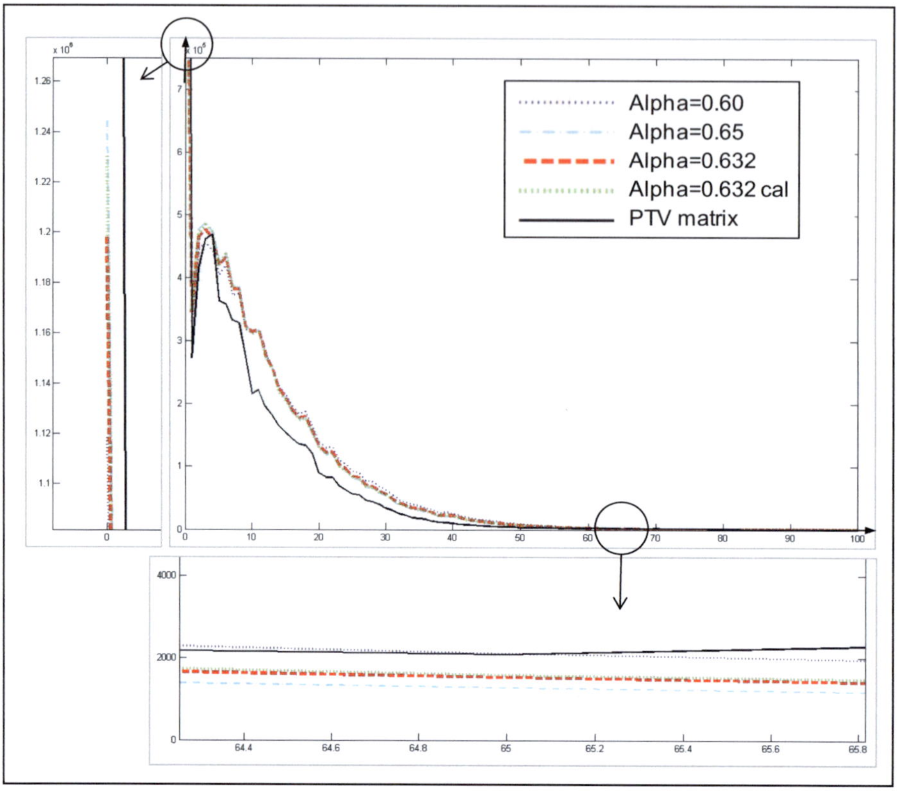

Figure 25: Distance distribution for various alphas in comparison to the non-business (altered) PTV passenger car matrix

A more complicated non-linear generalized cost function could probably balance the trip length distribution allowing for a better fit in terms of short- and long distances. This would, however, also involve a more complicated indirect loss calculation and more parameters to identify. Bearing in mind that the adjusted VALIDATE internal non-business O/D matrix is also an estimated matrix, and might therefore also show deviations to reality, and that the purpose of the logit model is to demonstrate the suggested loss calculation methodology in a comprehensible way, rather than displaying complicated up-to-date modeling techniques, the shortcomings from the under- and overestimation of trips of specific lengths are venial, as long as the assignment results have a similar acceptable traffic count fit as the original VALIDATE assignment. This is the case as will be described further below.

Another calibration is performed through the generalized costs in the logit model by entering the distance and duration matrices from the assignment procedure of the estimated model back into the logit model estimation. Figure 26 shows the development of the deviations to the VALIDATE time (dTij), distance (dDij), generalized cost (dCij) and adjusted internal non-business trip matrix (Tripsij) in the repetitive feedback cycle in and out of the logit model. Step 1 (on the x-axis) shows the deviations of the logit model, with the parameters mentioned above, and the duration and distance matrices from the original VALIDATE matrix assignment. 'Abs' represents the absolute deviation, 'perc' the deviation relative to the sum of all trips, minutes, kilometers or generalized costs, while 'avg' refers to the average deviation in respect to all ODs. Step 2 shows decreasing deviations in all figures, as here the time and distance matrices of the assignment including the estimated matrix of the logit model in step 1 are taken. For example, the average absolute deviation of the estimated to the VALIDATE passenger car matrix trips is ca. 7 in the first step, and decreases to ca. 6.7 in the second step. The repetition of the process leads to a lesser variability in deviations. The trips matrix and assignment results of step 3 are further taken as reference for the loss calculation. The corresponding distance distribution is also displayed in Figure 25, marked as '0.632 cal'.

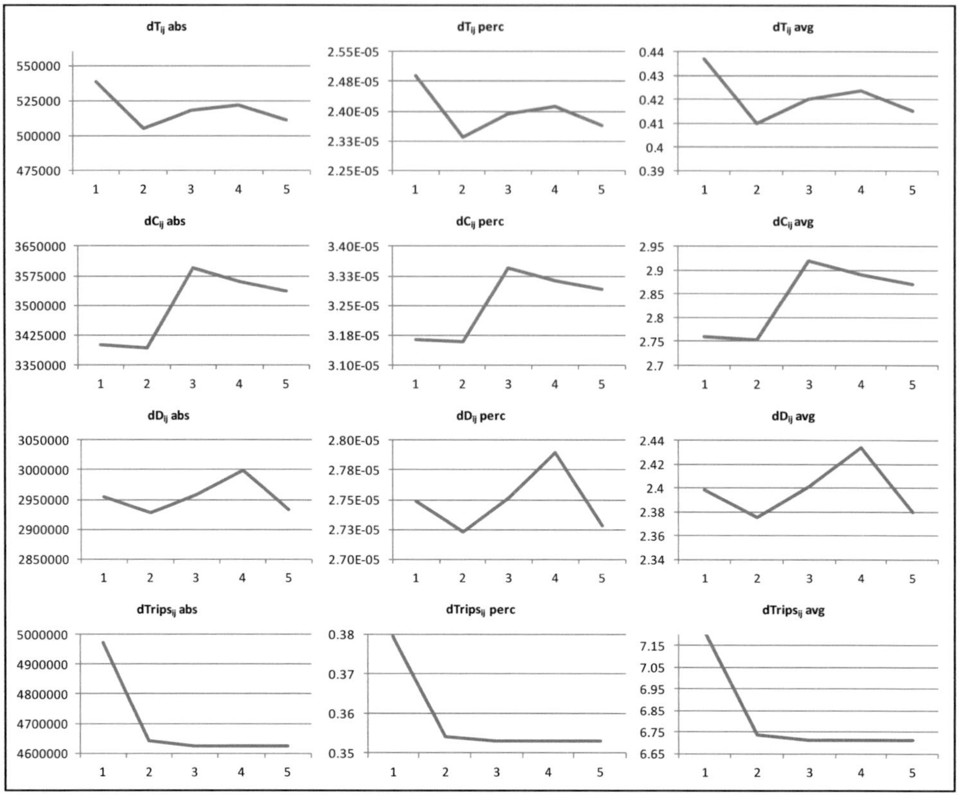

Figure 26: Deviations of the estimated matrices from the PTV passenger car trip (Tripsij) matrix, PTV time (Tij) and distance (Dij) skim matrices and their generalized costs (Cij) for each estimation procedure step

The traffic count fit of the original VALIDATE passenger car matrix (all purposes) and truck matrix is demonstrated in Figure 27 and Figure 28, with the estimated values on the y-axis and the traffic count values on the x-axis. The figures include some quality/correlation measures such as R^2 and mre, as well as the gradient (perfection would be a gradient of 1, when both lines lie exactly on each other). Figure 29 and Figure 30 show the traffic count fit of the passenger cars, including the (final) logit model-based estimated trips and the fit with trucks. For trucks, the assignment quality stays nearly the same. The fit of traffic counts with the passenger cars declines a bit when the logit-based non-business internal O/D matrix is included. The overall fit is, however, sufficiently accurate to proceed to the loss calculation and CI identification in the case study with the estimated parameters as they are.

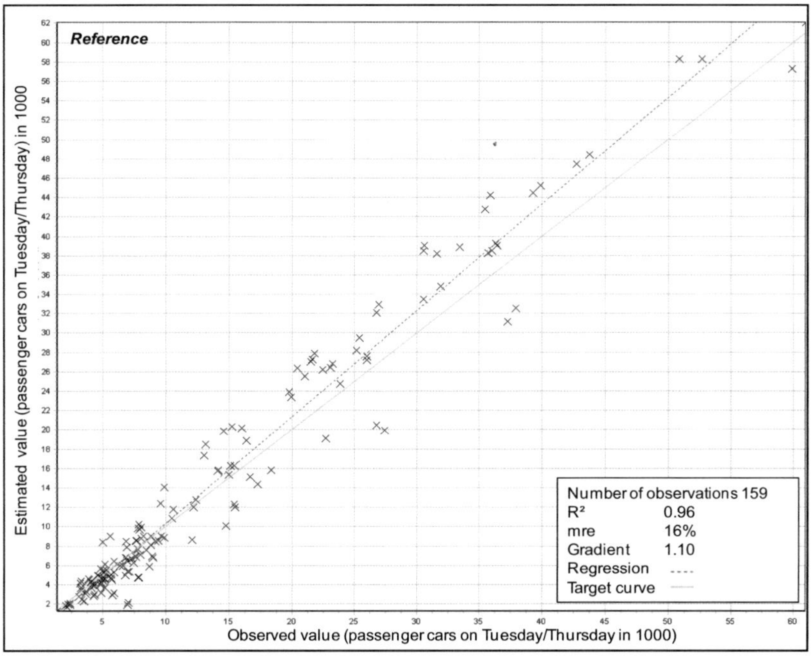

Figure 27: Estimated traffic (PTV Version) versus traffic count data for passenger cars

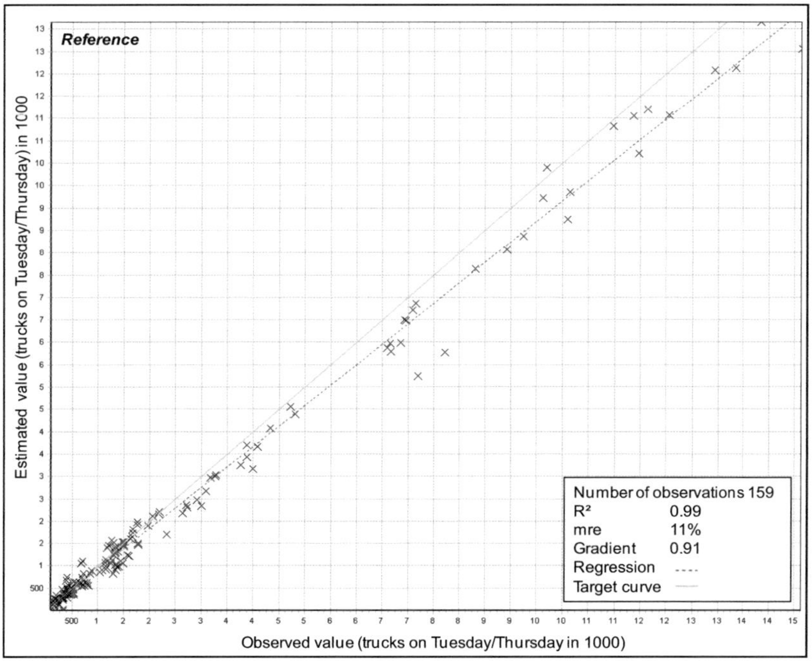

Figure 28: Estimated traffic (PTV Version) versus traffic count data for trucks

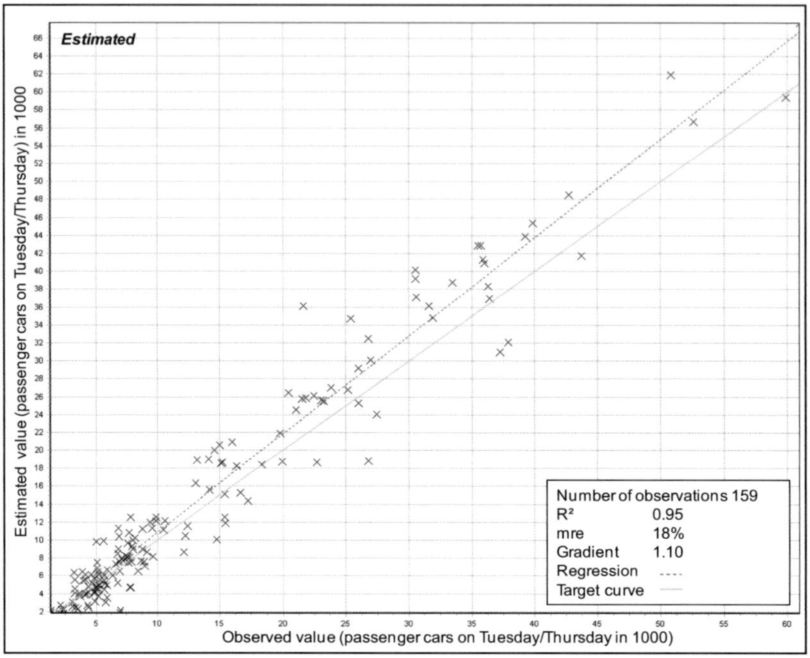

Figure 29: Estimated traffic (Logit model) versus traffic count data for passenger cars

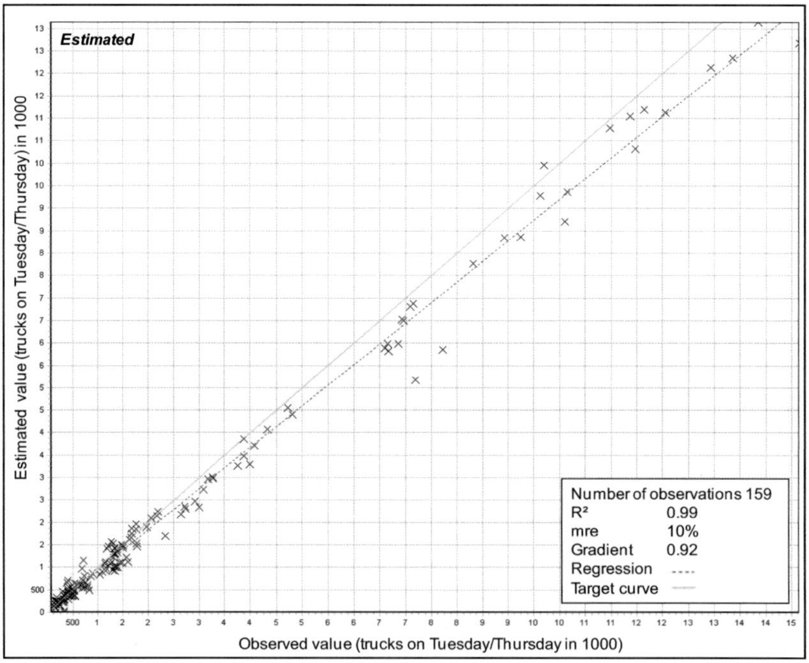

Figure 30: Estimated traffic (Logit model) versus traffic count data for trucks

4.5 Definition of the criticality threshold

The identification of CIs on the basis of the indirect loss values necessitates a threshold, above which road sections are considered to be critical (see Figure 3). The Directive 2008/114/EC "on the Identification and Designation of European Critical Infrastructure (ECI) and the Assessment of the Need to Improve their Protection" does not explicitly state a threshold value. Its determination is the responsibility of the member states. Depending on the purpose and the context of the CI identification, the determination of the threshold could follow different methodologies. Basically there are three options:

- **A preset number**, such as 1 million Euro: The preset number could be related to the gross domestic product (GDP) of the region or any other reference. For example, in a 0.1% relation to the GDP of Germany in 2005, the threshold is 2.242 billion Euro[45] which is much higher than any of the indirect losses calculated for Baden-Wuerttemberg in this case study. The same holds for 0.1% of Baden-Wuerttemberg's GDP in 2005, with 322.4 million Euro[46]. An advantage of this method is that the results can potentially be compared to other CI studies of, for example, other federal states.

- **Relative to other values**, such as with Jenks' natural breaks (Jenks (1967), p.187f): In this case, the threshold is determined based on the set of indirect loss values in the sample. This could be done using natural breaks. In a predefined number of clusters, the clusters' ranges are determined by minimizing the variance around the mean within a group, and maximizing it to the mean of other groups. This methodology takes into account the distribution of indirect loss potentials among the road section set. The number of CIs in the cluster with the highest indirect losses varies with the number of clusters the natural break methodology is performed on. An advantage of this approach is that, even with rather small differences in indirect losses, a clustering of road sections in more or less critical links is possible.

- **Fixed amount of CIs**, e.g. 10% of the road link set with the highest indirect loss potential: This methodology ignores the distribution of indirect losses. For example, if 1% of the road sections have an extremely high and 99% a marginal indirect loss potential, displaying the results of the highest 10% and identifying them as the most critical distort the

---

[45] Calculation based on Statistische Ämter des Bundes und der Länder (2011)
[46] Ibid.

view on CIs. Nevertheless it is a recommendable criterion if the road link set needs to be downsized for a more detailed analysis.

In the Baden-Wuerttemberg case study, the results of the two former approaches are juxtaposed. Five clusters differentiate the road sections according to their indirect loss potential. This number of clusters allows differentiating the results to a certain degree of detail, but keeps the classes at a manageable level. Figure 31 shows a schematic picture of the criticality classes. Red stands for the most critical links with the highest loss potential. Orange, yellow, green and grey-green represent the graduated loss classes. The preset cluster ranges for the indirect losses are defined based on the order of magnitude of the indirect losses calculated, and meet at 250, 500, 750, 1000 thousand Euro. The cluster ranges for natural breaks are calculated based on the relevant data within the ArcGIS software. The number of sections within one cluster varies with the clustering approach. Therefore this number will be displayed next to the cluster range legend in the relevant figures in Chapter 5.

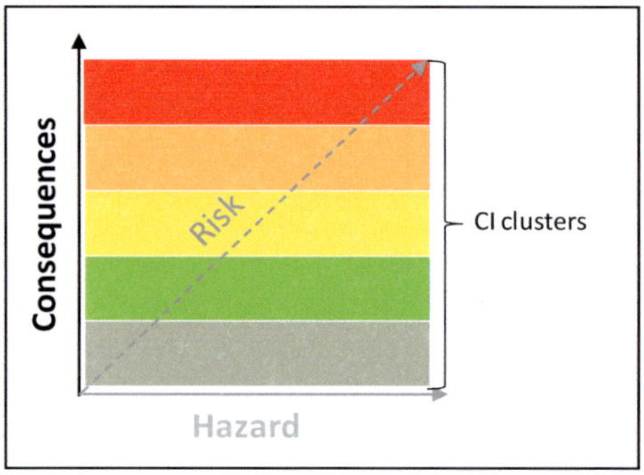

Figure 31: Identification of CI clusters

4.6 MEASURES FOR ANALYZING THE RESULTS

In order to analyze associations between the criticality ranking respectively the indirect losses and other rankings based on variables such as the number of vehicles, the correlation between the variables need to be tested. Depending on the type of variables (metric or ordinal) and the questions behind the correlation testing various correlation coefficients may be applied. The relevant correlation measures for analyzing the results of the case study are presented here and find their application in Chapter 5.

The correlation of two metric variables is typically measured by Pearson's correlation coefficient. It captures the linear relationship of two variables x and y and is defined as (Bol (2004b), p.186):

$$r = \frac{Cov(x,y)}{\sqrt{Var(x) \cdot Var(y)}}, 0 \leq |r| \leq 1 \tag{4-10}$$

It corresponds to the covariance of the two variables x and y divided by the product of their standard deviations and may be construed as (Cleff (2008), p.110):

$$|r| < 0.5 \quad small\ linear\ association$$

$$0.5 \leq |r| < 0.8 \quad medium\ linear\ association$$

$$|r| \geq 0.8 \quad large\ linear\ association$$

The advantage of Pearson's correlation coefficient is that the distances between the ranks are taken into account. However, outliers may distort the results significantly, and only linear associations can be traced. Monotonous associations are captured in Spearman's (r^s) and Kendall-tau (τ) rank correlation coefficients. These two concepts are applied to ordinal variables or metric variables put into a ranking according to their order. In contrast to τ, the assumption in r^s is of an equidistance between the rank positions of a variable, which makes τ a less restricted concept. (Cleff (2008))

Spearman's rank correlation coefficient r^s ($-1 \leq r^S \leq 1$) is defined as (Bol (2004a), p.144):

$$r^s = 1 - \frac{6 \cdot \sum_{i=1}^{n} \left(R_x(i) - R_y(i)\right)^2}{n \cdot (n^2 - 1)}, \quad 0 \leq |r^s| \leq 1 \tag{4-11}$$

n *number of road sections*

$R_x(i)$ *Rank of road section i in the ranking based on variable x*

$R_y(i)$ *Rank of road section i in the ranking based on variable y*

It may be interpreted as:

$$r^s \approx -1 \quad trend\ in\ the\ opposite\ direction$$

$$r^s \approx 0 \quad no\ trend\ observable$$

$$r^s \approx 1 \quad trend\ in\ the\ same\ direction$$

Kendall-tau τ measures the proportion of disarray between a sorted reference ranking of a variable and the ranking of the variable to compare it with. It only takes into account if the disarray of two rank positions is positive, negative or zero, no matter the distance between the rank positions. T is defined as τ_a in case of no ties[47] in the data sets, and τ_b if ties exist (Cleff (2008), p.121):

$$\tau_a = \frac{P-I}{\frac{1}{2}n\cdot(n-1)}, 0 \leq |\tau_a| \leq 1 \quad (4\text{-}12)$$

$$\tau_b = \frac{P-I}{\sqrt{\left(\frac{1}{2}n\cdot(n-1)-T\right)\left(\frac{1}{2}n\cdot(n-1)-U\right)}}, \quad 0 \leq |\tau_b| \leq 1 \quad (4\text{-}13)$$

n	*number of road sections*
P	*number of concordant pairs*
I	*number of discordant pairs*
T	*length of ties of variable x*
U	*length of ties of variable y*

Since τ neglects the absolute differences between the rank positions, another indicator, the average shift in rank positions $\bar{R}$, adds to the whole interpretation of the analysis. It is calculated as the average of the absolute differences in road sections' ranking with respect to a ranking based on different variables (Nardo et al. (2005), p. 82):[48]

$$\bar{R} = \frac{1}{n}\sum_{i=1}^{n}|R_x(i) - R_y(i)| \quad (4\text{-}14)$$

4.7 Recapitulation of the case study's approach

This chapter explained the assumptions, restrictions and model estimation steps required for the indirect loss and criticality assessment in the Baden-Wuerttemberg case study. An available extract version of the transport model VALIDATE was combined with a self estimated logit model representing the destination choice step for non-business trips. This allows the performance of the calculations on a detailed network with a professional computational

---

47 'Ties' exist when values or rankings appear more than once.

48 Except for the average shift in rank positions $\bar{R}$, which is calculated using Microsoft Excel 'by hand', all coefficients are readily available for calculation in the PASW Statistics 18 software (now called: IBM® SPSS® Statistics).

background for the trip assignment through VALIDATE while, at the same time, being able to transparently demonstrate the loss calculation methodology with the logit model. The monetization largely conforms to the cost-benefit scheme of the German National Transport Infrastructure Plan from 2003, with necessary adjustments (e.g. price levels, purpose differentiation, etc.) and simplifications (e.g. flat treatment of external costs). For a criticality assessment, a threshold needs to be defined, above which infrastructures are considered as critical. This chapter presented three general possibilities to derive such a threshold, of which two will be applied in the case study. Furthermore, relevant correlation measures and an indicator representing the average shift in rank positions were explained in more detail in order to be able to later analyze the indirect loss calculation results and criticality assessment more deeply.

5 BADEN-WUERTTEMBERG CASE STUDY: RESULTS

5.1 CRITICAL ROAD SECTIONS IN BADEN-WUERTTEMBERG DUE TO INDIRECT LOSS POTENTIAL

5.1.1 INDIRECT LOSSES AND CRITICALITY RANKING

Applying the indirect loss calculation methodology described in Chapters 3 and 4, each of the 296 motorway sections in Baden-Wuerttemberg holds a short- and medium-term indirect loss potential in the event of its interruption.

Figure 32 outlines the indirect short-term losses including external costs with thresholds based on preset values (left) and natural breaks (right). The values range between ca. 2,000 and 2,000,000 Euro per day. The highest losses, and therefore the most critical links, are in the region of Stuttgart. The close up in Figure 33 identifies the section from Kreuz Stuttgart to Stuttgart-Möhringen as the most critical one, with short-term indirect losses of 2,010,147 Euro per day. The section in the reverse direction is nearly as critical with 1,896,654 Euro per day short-term indirect losses. In proportion to the economic performance of Baden-Wuerttemberg, the maximum losses correspond to ca. 0.2% of the average daily GDP. The number of vehicles affected by a closure of the section from Kreuz Stuttgart to Stuttgart-Möhringen or reverse amounts to ca. 1.1 million passenger and freight vehicles per day, which corresponds to ca. 8% of all vehicles travelling in the network. The affected vehicles are not necessarily vehicles that previously used the now closed road section. Affected vehicles are also those that experience more traffic on their original routes due to the detours of others.

The link with the third highest indirect losses connects Esslingen with Stuttgart-Plieningen. About 950,000 vehicles would be affected here. The travelers in the Stuttgart-Rohr, Stuttgart-Möhringen, Wendlingen and Leinfelden-Echterdingen regions, as well as in the cordon zones originating in Wörth (west of Karlsruhe) and east of Ulm (also including traffic from Munich), experience the highest degradation in their travel utilities due to the closure of one of the three links associated with the highest indirect short-term losses. This shows that the nearby regions are not only affected by the reduced access to the motorways, but also with detouring vehicles. The cordon zones are affected because they inject high traffic loads. This is also the explanation for why the origins and destinations with the greatest rise in travel disutilities for all of their travelers are, in both directions, the cordon zones close to Ulm and Mannheim, as well as Ulm and Karlsruhe.

The application of the two threshold setting methodologies induces different overall pictures of the criticality level within Baden-Wuerttemberg. The thresholds with preset values (Figure 32, left) mark only 2% of links being very critical (red), and a large majority (85%) as being rather uncritical (grey and green) compared to the other links. The thresholds based on natural breaks (Figure 32, right) offer a more balanced picture, with 4% very critical links (red), 64% uncritical links (grey and green) and the rest of links in between these. Hence, it is crucial to interpret the resulting criticality pictures against the background of the indirect loss values and the threshold setting methodology.

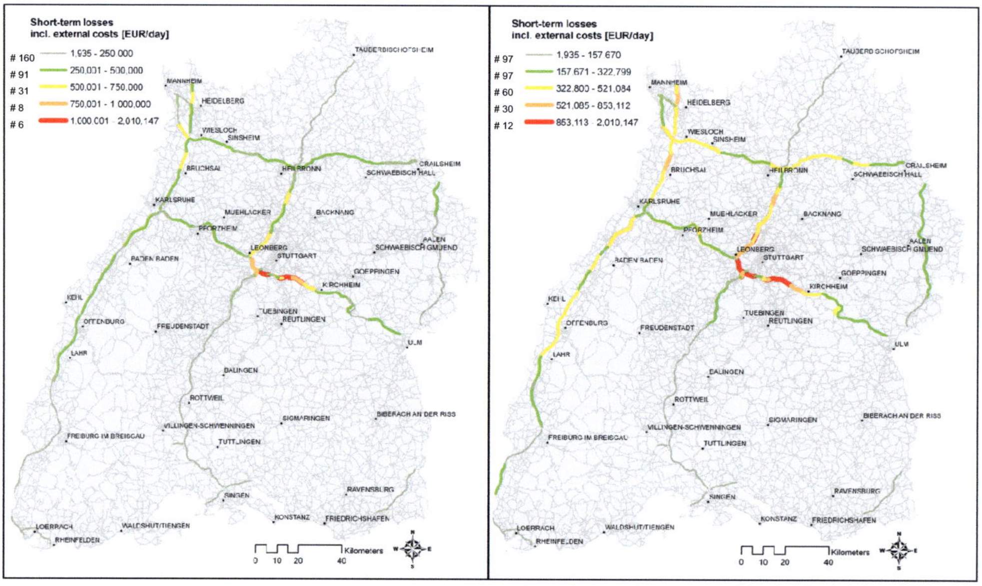

Figure 32: Short-term indirect losses including external costs [EUR/day] with preset thresholds (left) and natural breaks (right)

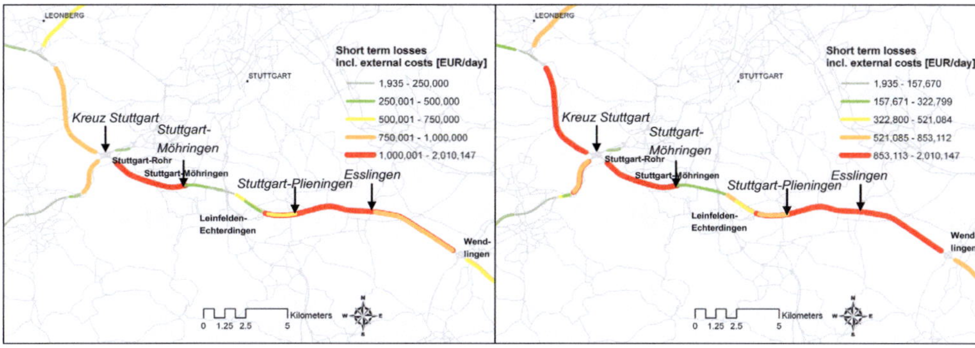

Figure 33: Short-term indirect losses including external costs [EUR/day] with preset thresholds (left) and natural breaks (right) for the region of Stuttgart

Looking at the medium-term and short-term losses excluding external costs in Figure 34, a significant difference is not observable. The losses overall decrease, but the criticality ranking looks very similar. In fact, a closer look at the data validates this observation. Calculating the correlation measures and the average shift in rank positions, the expected short-term indirect losses correlate significantly with the medium-term losses and so do their rankings (see Table 12). Their average shift in rank positions, $\bar{R}$, is 1.03. Looking at the 30 most critical links based on short-term losses, the $\bar{R}$ rises to 1.13. The most critical three links in respect of short-term losses equal the ones related to medium-term losses. Consequently, it does not make a significant difference in terms of the criticality ranking if destination choice changes are taken into account or not, at least for the case of the motorways in Baden-Wuerttemberg. It matters, however, when looking at the absolute indirect losses for, for example, the justification of risk management measures.

Another interesting question is whether or not the short-term loss reduction potential due to destination choice changes in the medium-term correlates with the number of affected vehicles (all vehicles directly or indirectly concerned with the road closure) or with the short-term losses. Put another way, do more critical links based on short-term losses show a trend towards a higher loss reduction potential in the medium-term, and has the number of overall affected vehicles anything to do with the criticality rankings related to short-term losses, or with the loss reduction potential in the medium-term. Table 13 summarizes the correlation measures. Accordingly, all correlations are significant. However, the strength of the trend differs. The affected vehicles show a medium to strong correlation with the short-term losses, with an average shift in rank positions, $\bar{R}$, of 41, while their link to the medium-term loss reduction potential is only medium to low.

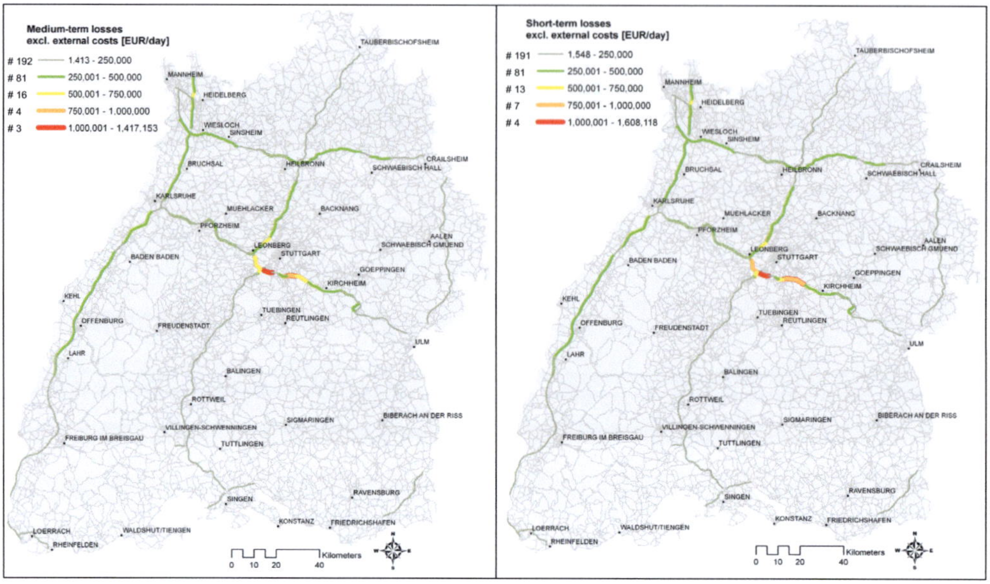

Figure 34: Medium-term and short-term indirect losses excluding external costs [EUR/day] with preset thresholds

N=296			(Ranking) time costs	(Ranking) distance-based costs	(Ranking) short-term losses	(Ranking) medium-term losses
Kendall-Tau-b	Ranking time costs	Correlation coefficient	1	.202**	.958**	.955**
		Sig. (2-sided)	.	,000	,000	,000
	Ranking-distance based costs	Correlation coefficient	.202**	1	.244**	.246**
		Sig. (2-sided)	,000	.	,000	,000
	Ranking short-term losses	Correlation coefficient	.958**	.244**	1	.992**
		Sig. (2-sided)	,000	,000	.	,000
	Ranking medium-term losses	Correlation coefficient	.955**	.246**	.992**	1
		Sig. (2-sided)	,000	,000	,000	.
Spearman-Rho	Ranking time costs	Correlation coefficient	1	.273**	.997**	.996**
		Sig. (2-sided)	.	,000	,000	,000
	Ranking-distance based costs	Correlation coefficient	.273**	1	.332**	.336**
		Sig. (2-sided)	,000	.	,000	,000
	Ranking short-term losses	Correlation coefficient	.997**	.332**	1	1.000**
		Sig. (2-sided)	,000	,000	.	,000
	Ranking medium-term losses	Correlation coefficient	.996**	.336**	1.000**	1
		Sig. (2-sided)	,000	,000	,000	.
Pearson	time costs	Correlation coefficient	1	.225**	.998**	.996**
		Sig. (2-sided)	.	,000	,000	,000
	distance-based costs	Correlation coefficient	.225**	1	.279**	.284**
		Sig. (2-sided)	,000	.	,000	,000
	short-term losses	Correlation coefficient	.998**	.279**	1	.997**
		Sig. (2-sided)	,000	,000	.	,000
	medium-term losses	Correlation coefficient	.996**	.284**	.997**	1
		Sig. (2-sided)	,000	,000	,000	.

** The correlation is significant on a level of 0.01 (two sided).

Table 12: Correlation between the criticality ranking based on short-, medium-term losses, distance-based costs and time costs

N=296			(Ranking) affected vehicles	(Ranking) medium-term loss reduction [%]	(Ranking) short-term losses
Kendall-Tau-b	Ranking affected vehicles	Correlation coefficient	1	.434**	.627**
		Sig. (2-sided)	.	.000	.000
	Ranking medium-term loss reduction [%]	Correlation coefficient	.434**	1	.320**
		Sig. (2-sided)	.000	.	.000
	Ranking short-term losses	Correlation coefficient	.627**	.320**	1
		Sig. (2-sided)	.000	.000	.
Spearman-Rho	Ranking affected vehicles	Correlation coefficient	1	.582**	.813**
		Sig. (2-sided)	.	.000	.000
	Ranking medium-term loss reduction [%]	Correlation coefficient	.582**	1	.441**
		Sig. (2-sided)	.000	.	.000
	Ranking short-term losses	Correlation coefficient	.813**	.441**	1
		Sig. (2-sided)	.000	.000	.
Pearson	affected vehicles	Correlation coefficient	1	.573**	.808**
		Sig. (2-sided)	.	.000	.000
	medium-term loss reduction [%]	Correlation coefficient	.573**	1	.654**
		Sig. (2-sided)	.000	.	.000
	short-term losses	Correlation coefficient	.808**	.654**	1
		Sig. (2-sided)	.000	.000	.

** The correlation is significant on a level of 0.01 (two sided).

Table 13: Correlation between the criticality ranking based on short-term losses, affected vehicles and medium-term loss reduction [%] on short-term losses

The cost components in the short-term losses are dependent on the additional time and distance due to detours, as well as the assessment parameters VOT and VOD. As can be seen in Figure 35 and Figure 36, the time costs highly dominate the distance-based costs. On some road sections there is even the potential to save operating costs due to detours with fewer kilometers. This is not surprising. For instance, GPS navigators leave users the option to choose the quickest or shortest route, and usually these routes are not the same. Since the calculation of operating costs foregoes the differentiation by speed, congested roads only influence the duration of travel visible in the time costs, but not in the operating costs. Table 12 attests the significant strong correlation between time costs and short-term losses. The average shift in rank positions, $\bar{R}$, amounts to 4.6 for all road sections, and only 1.0 for the 30 road sections with the highest indirect short-term losses. The correlation measures between the short-term losses and the distance-based costs show only a statistically significant minor linear trend. The same holds for the correlation of the distance-based and time costs.

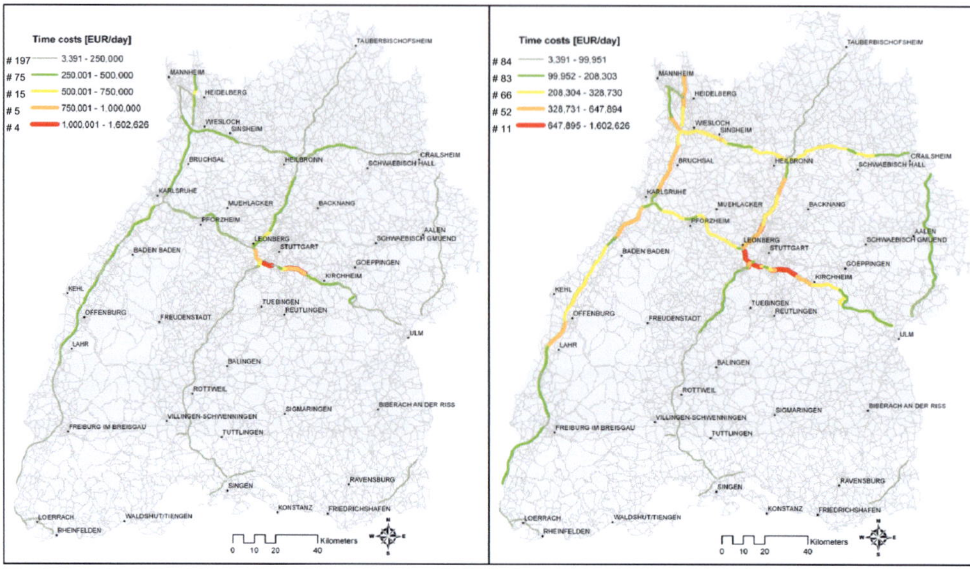

Figure 35: Short-term time costs [EUR/day] related to detours with preset thresholds (left) and natural breaks (right)

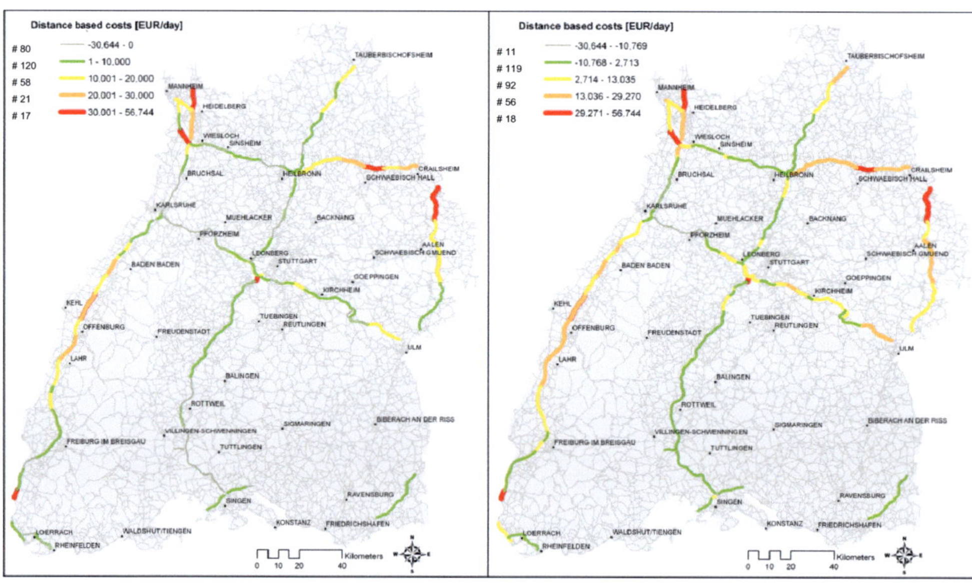

Figure 36: Short-term distance-based costs [EUR/day] related to detours with preset thresholds (left) and natural breaks (right)

As time costs contribute significantly to the indirect losses, and thus to the criticality ranking, they need to undergo a further analysis. In order to test the ranking's robustness in respect of the underlying VOT assessment approach, the short-term losses based on the VOTold and

VOTnew, as presented in section 4.3.1, are compared. As can be seen in Table 14, the criticality rankings based on the short-term losses calculated using the VOTold and the VOTnew correlate significantly with an average shift in rank positions of 2.48. The $\bar{R}$ of the 30 most critical links is 1.13, which certifies the ranking as being more robust for the links with high indirect losses. Since the motorway sections under consideration have a length of ca. 10km on average, it is unlikely that a detour takes less than 5 minutes longer than the original route, unless there is a parallel road with similar capacity. Thus, the rise in the valuation of travel time differences of more than five minutes in the VOTnew applies equally to the majority of links, and therefore entails no significant change in the ranking. However, the absolute values of indirect losses differ for the two VOTs. When applying the VOTnew, the short-term losses increase on average by 1.3%. Compared to the 30 most critical links based on the short-term losses using the VOTold, the short-term losses using the VOTnew are ca. 7% higher, which corresponds to an absolute short-term loss increase on average by ca. 67,623 Euro. The two most critical links based on the VOTnew are the same as with the application of the VOTold, but the absolute short-term losses are 2,192,250 Euro and 2,078,713 Euro. This is ca. 180,000 Euro higher compared to the short-term losses based on the VOTold. Consequently, it is recommended to use both of the values, on the one hand to demonstrate the robustness of the ranking and on the other hand to show the range of indirect losses that can be expected when varying the VOT.

N=296			(Ranking) short-term losses VOTold	(Ranking) short-term losses VOTnew
Kendall-Tau-b	Ranking short-term losses VOTold	Correlation coefficient	1	.979**
		Sig. (2-sided)	.	.000
	Ranking short-term losses VOTnew	Correlation coefficient	.979**	1
		Sig. (2-sided)	.000	.
Spearman-Rho	Ranking short-term losses VOTold	Correlation coefficient	1	.999**
		Sig. (2-sided)	.	.000
	Ranking short-term losses VOTnew	Correlation coefficient	.999**	1
		Sig. (2-sided)	.000	.
Pearson	Short-term losses VOTold	Correlation coefficient	1	.999**
		Sig. (2-sided)	.	.000
	Short-term losses VOTnew	Correlation coefficient	.999**	1
		Sig. (2-sided)	.000	.

** The correlation is significant on a level of 0,01 (two sided).

Table 14: Correlation between the criticality ranking based on short-term losses with the VOTold and VOTnew

5.1.2 Correlation between the criticality ranking and rankings of external variables

The easiest, probably cheapest and apparently most common way to identify critical road sections is to derive the ranking based on the number of vehicles on the road sections under consideration. This could be done through the use of traffic count data. In terms of consistency to the indirect loss calculation and criticality identification applied here, the number of modeled vehicles on the road sections is used for comparison. It turns out that there is a significant positive correlation between the number of vehicles and the short term losses related to the road sections (see Table 15). The correlation is, however, only on a medium level (according to Cleff (2008), p.110). The $\bar{R}$ of 38.68 for all and 24.0 for the 30 most critical links supports this rating. Consequently, the number of vehicles may be applied to approximate a criticality ranking based on indirect losses, the approximation is, however, on a very rough level. Considering the costs and time for the implementation of a transport model and the indirect loss calculation, the approximation using the number of vehicles is definitely a viable procedure for identifying critical road infrastructures for practitioners. Yet, lacking monetization, this approach does not help in justifying spending in risk management measures.

N=296			(Ranking) vehicles	(Ranking) short-term losses
Kendall-Tau-b	Ranking vehicles	Correlation coefficient	1	.633**
		Sig. (2-sided)	.	.000
	Ranking short-term losses	Correlation coefficient	.633**	1
		Sig. (2-sided)	.000	.
Spearman-Rho	Ranking vehicles	Correlation coefficient	1	.811**
		Sig. (2-sided)	.	.000
	Ranking short-term losses	Correlation coefficient	.811**	1
		Sig. (2-sided)	.000	.
Pearson	vehicles	Correlation coefficient	1	.730**
		Sig. (2-sided)	.	.000
	Short-term losses	Correlation coefficient	.730**	1
		Sig. (2-sided)	.000	.

** The correlation is significant on a level of 0,01 (two sided).

Table 15: Correlation between the criticality ranking based on short-term losses and numbers of vehicles

One might argue that the length of the road sections highly influences its criticality, as a long section potentially requires longer detours if no similar parallel roads exist. Thus, there is no correlation observable with the short-term indirect losses (see Table 16). The $\bar{R}$ of 96.13 evidences a high variation in the rankings.

N=296			(Ranking) length	(Ranking) short-term losses
Kendall-Tau-b	Ranking length	Correlation coefficient	1	.047
		Sig. (2-sided)	.	.231
	Ranking short-term losses	Correlation coefficient	.047	1
		Sig. (2-sided)	.231	.
Spearman-Rho	Ranking length	Correlation coefficient	1	.076
		Sig. (2-sided)	.	.194
	Ranking short-term losses	Correlation coefficient	.076	1
		Sig. (2-sided)	.194	.
Pearson	length	Correlation coefficient	1	.076
		Sig. (2-sided)	.	.194
	Short-term losses	Correlation coefficient	.076	1
		Sig. (2-sided)	.194	.

Table 16: Correlation between the criticality ranking based on short-term losses and road length

5.1.3 THE INDIRECT LOSSES IN THE CONTEXT OF BONUS/MALUS PAYMENTS OF CONSTRUCTION SITES

There is hardly any possibility of comparing the order of magnitude of the calculated indirect losses with other sources. Bonus/malus payments with regard to road infrastructures' construction sites compensate/penalize the building company for earlier/later completion of a construction site. An earlier/later completion entails lower/higher indirect costs imposed on the road users. Hence these payments have at least an imaginary connection to the indirect costs calculated in this study, and therefore here serve as source for comparison.

Capacity reductions due to construction sites are similar to disruptions due to other reasons (e.g. an accident) as focused on in this study. The main distinction is that construction sites are planned and foreseeable, and serve for the purpose of the improvement of the original situation. Rerouting alternatives (e.g. the temporary reallocation of one of the lanes in the opposite direction) are organized beforehand, and communicated. Hardly ever do construction sites on motorways lead to a complete closure in one direction. Sudden, unplanned interruptions due to natural events or accidents cause greater confusion for travelers and a stronger intervention in travel plans. The flexible reallocation of one or more lanes in the opposite direction is not always quickly possible. Nevertheless, both situations are characterized by capacity reductions.

Federal and federal states' road construction authorities allow for a bonus/malus system in respect to the duration of construction works as stated in their handbook on the awarding of contracts and the execution of road and bridge construction works (HVA B-StB) (BMVBS

(2010a), 04/10, 1.3 (11)-(15)). Examples of the application of the system can be found in Bavaria and North Rhine-Westfalia (Waha (2009); Landesbetrieb Straßenbau Nordrhein-Westfalen (2006)). Bonus payments in the event of earlier completion of construction works are so far exceptions and underlie discussions with regard to their justification. Contracts should be designed to reduce the duration of the degradation of serviceability to a reasonable level, always taking into account the costs and benefits related to it. A bonus payment therefore assumes that there is still optimization potential in the contract design. From an economic perspective, society saves or loses indirect costs with an earlier or delayed completion of works in respect to the degradation of serviceability. Incentivizing contractors to exceed their expected productivity set in the contract by letting them participate in society's benefits, seems reasonable. However, the bonus/malus payments connected to a one day acceleration/delay of capacity reductions are not calculated according to the indirect loss calculation presented here. They are rather derived as a percentage of the direct costs of the construction works[49].

Looking at the concrete values given in the handbook HVA B-StB (04/10, 1.3, p.13) there is no case of a complete closure in one direction without reallocation of at least one lane in the opposite direction – which would be necessary to compare with the indirect short-term losses calculated here. Taking the most critical road section in respect to short-term losses from Kreuz Stuttgart to Stuttgart-Möhringen, the degradation of serviceability due to construction works costs 1,550-38,350 Euro per day, depending on how many lanes have to be closed and if the other direction is also affected[50]. These costs correspond to ca. 0.1 to 2 % of the indirect losses including external costs, based on a complete closure calculated in this study. The discrepancy between the values can be explained by the different degree of closure assumed in the study and referenced in the handbook, as well as by the background of the derivation of the handbook's values. But it may also hint that future bonus/malus payments could gain in importance and size.

[49] Carreno et al. (2007) also suggest expressing indirect effects as fraction of the physical effects. Accordingly, indirect effects cannot exceed the physical effects. However, the existence of an empirical proof of such a relation is still missing and it is doubtful if such a relation also holds for CIs.

[50] The calculation is based on daily traffic values (DTV) 2005 published in Straßenbauverwaltung Baden-Württemberg (2007), northern part.

5.2 Critical road sections with high disruption potential

Following a criticality investigation, a recommendation as to how to protect designated infrastructures is often called for. This requires an examination of possible hazardous events leading to a disruption of service, and hence a derivation of the risk level. In order to draw an (indirect) risk map based on the indirect cost estimation results, information on the probability of road failure is essential. Hazard and vulnerability maps exist for all kinds of natural events. However, the captured vulnerability usually only refers to residential buildings. Vulnerability maps in respect to the serviceability of roads can rarely be found.

For the purpose of this study, one map on the susceptibility to failure (multi-hazard) and one map on the flooding probability with regard to motorway sections are available. Their characteristics and the results of their combination with the indirect loss potential are demonstrated and discussed in the following paragraphs. Some studies assume a closure probability proportional to the road link's length (e.g. Jenelius (2007a); Jenelius (2009)). This assumption cannot be supported in the case of Baden-Wuerttemberg, as shown later.

The (restricted) map on the susceptibility to failure of motorways on the state's territory results from a study commissioned by the Ministry of Environment, Nature Conservation and Transport of the Federal State of Baden-Wuerttemberg (SSP Consult (2003)). The four stage ordinal scale of the road sections' rating varies between "very high susceptibility to failure" and "very low susceptibility to failure". Translating this into risk terms, the susceptibility to failure is a mixture of hazard and vulnerability, since it contains the probability of an event that causes a reduction of serviceability. The basis of this study are surveys on congestion hot spots distributed among road offices, the analysis of warning messages referring to motorways, accident statistics, as well as theoretical instabilities (SSP Consult (2003), p.10). Although (regular) congestion itself is not considered to be an unexpected event and cause of failure in the calculation model of indirect losses, the map retrieved from the susceptibility study may be considered as a multi-hazard/vulnerability map and, in combination with the indirect cost calculations, helps to point out road sections under (indirect) risk.

Figure 37 classifies the susceptibility to failure categories and the short-term losses including external costs into risk levels. Since the hazard categories are not associated with exact probabilities, the risk classification is only qualitative and ranges from very low to very high. Figure 38 illustrates Baden Wuerttemberg's motorway sections with their respective indirect loss risk levels. The A5 north of Freiburg up to Mannheim, the A6 between Mannheim and

Crailsheim, the A8 between Karlsruhe and Stuttgart, as well as the A81 between Heilbronn and Stuttgart, are on a similar medium risk level. The A8 between Leonberg and Kirchheim faces the highest indirect loss risk. These sections exhibit high traffic loads and regular traffic jams due to, for example, accidents and commuter traffic. The A81 north of Heilbronn and south of Stuttgart, as well as the A5 south of Freiburg, show the lowest risk levels. It can therefore be stated that the motorway sections in less populated regions are exposed to less indirect loss risk than the more populated regions around Karlsruhe, Mannheim, Stuttgart and Heilbronn.

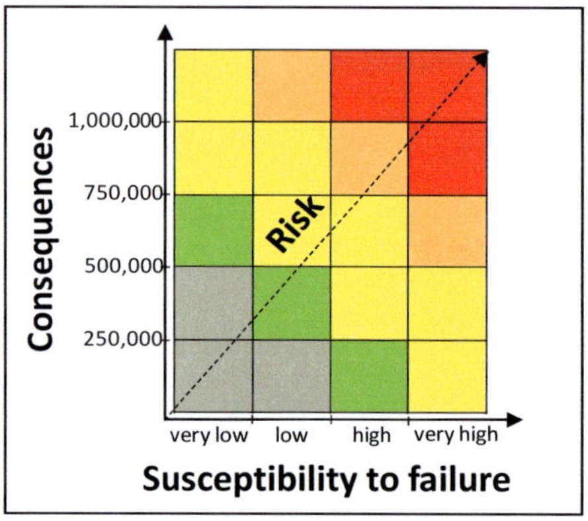

Figure 37: Risk classification based on short-term indirect losses incl. external costs and susceptibility to failure

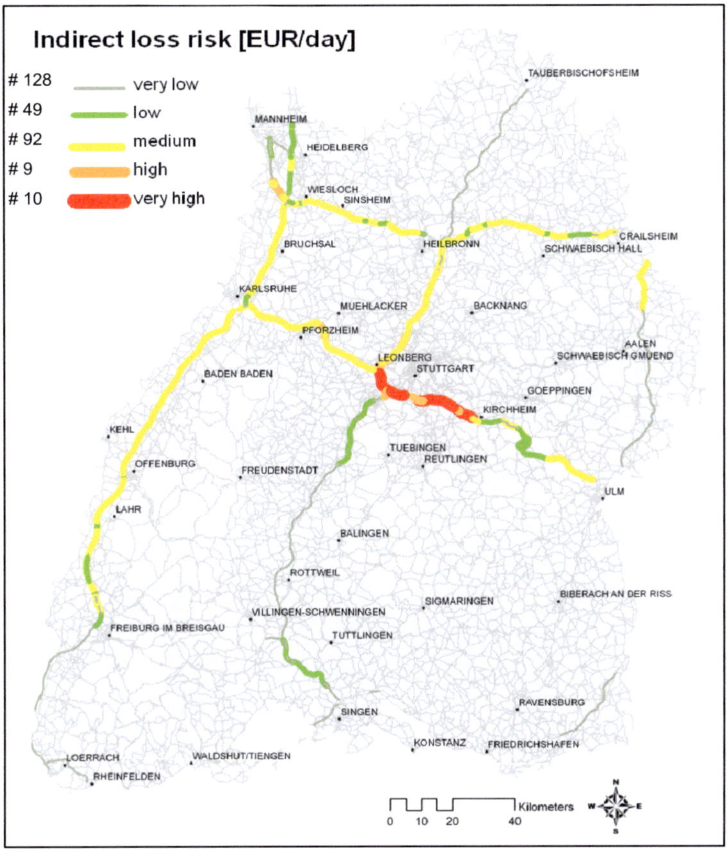

Figure 38: Indirect loss risk [EUR/day] based on short-term indirect losses incl. external costs and susceptibility to failure

The four most critical links from a short-term indirect loss perspective happen to also hold the highest level of susceptibility to failure, and therefore induce the highest indirect loss risk. This can be explained by the input parameters in the derivation of the susceptibility to failure. Congestion hot spots are likely to be located at road sections with many users and low detouring possibilities. The same characteristics also aggravate the short-term indirect losses. Therefore, this collision is not surprising. Apart from this obvious interconnection for the highest levels of hazard and consequences, there is only a minor correlation between them on lower levels.

Looking at the susceptibility to failure data, a significant correlation between the length of a road section and its failure probability is not identifiable (see Table 17). Accordingly, for Baden-Wuerttemberg, the length should not be taken as an estimator for road closure probabilities.

N=296			Susceptibility to failure	length
Kendall-Tau-b	Susceptibility to failure	Correlation coefficient	1	.046
		Sig. (2-sided)	.	.285
	length	Correlation coefficient	.046	1
		Sig. (2-sided)	.285	.
Spearman-Rho	Susceptibility to failure	Correlation coefficient	1	.062
		Sig. (2-sided)	.	.286
	length	Correlation coefficient	.062	1
		Sig. (2-sided)	.286	.
Pearson	Susceptibility to failure	Correlation coefficient	1	.066
		Sig. (2-sided)	.	.255
	length	Correlation coefficient	.066	1
		Sig. (2-sided)	.255	.

Table 17: Correlation coefficients for the length and susceptibility to failure of road sections

As mentioned in section 2.2.1, Baden-Wuerttemberg's motorways have already been affected by floods such as the one of August 2007 with regard to the A5 close to Freiburg (Spiegel Online GmbH (2007)). It is likely that something like this will similarly reoccur somewhere in Baden-Wuerttemberg, and that the serviceability of the affected road section will be partly or completely restricted. It is therefore of great interest to identify the road sections possibly affected, and the expected indirect losses coming along. For the purpose of this study, the motorway network and the flood hazard zones of ZÜRS Geo were overlapped. ZÜRS Geo has been developed by the German Insurance Association (GDV) and offers (re-) insurance companies an online platform displaying flood areas according to the following classification:

- Hazard Class 1: statistically less seldom than once every 200 years
- Hazard Class 2: statistically once every 50-200 years
- Hazard Class 3: statistically once every 10-50 years
- Hazard Class 4: statistically once every 10 years

The platform contains flood zoning data of more than 200 public water authorities and about 200,000 rivers (GDV (2008)). For this study, the motorway links obtained a flood hazard classification according to the ZÜRS flood hazard class at their location (see Figure 39). In the situation in which a link lies within two different zones, the higher hazard class value was assigned. The ZÜRS zones neglect the existence of bridges, entailing an overestimation of the actual flood hazard. Consequently, separate categories for road sections with bridges[51] are introduced.

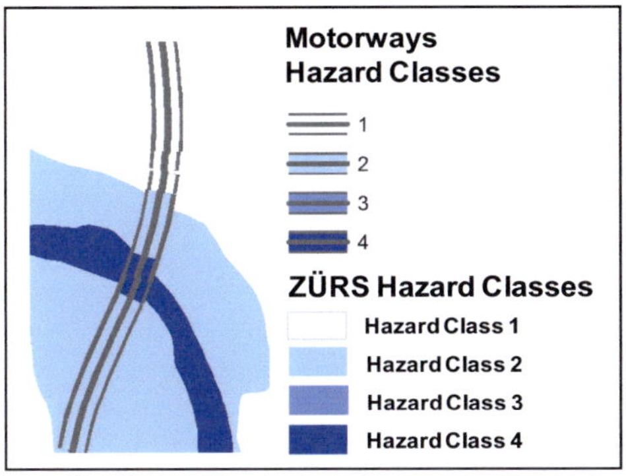

Figure 39: Example of flood hazard classification of motorway sections according to ZÜRS Hazard Classes

In order to obtain the risk related to indirect losses of the motorway sections, the hazard (= probability of failure) is multiplied by the expected indirect losses due to a failure. Assuming that a flood takes two days to subside, the indirect short-term losses including external costs associated with a two day disruption are determined and multiplied by the maximum hazard class relevant for the road section. In case of hazard class 1, or the existence of bridges (see explanation in previous paragraph), or no available data, the probability is set to zero. An event on a road section of hazard class 4 happens with a probability of 0.1 per year (corresponds to statistically once every 10 years). For hazard class 3, the probability assigned is 0.02 per year (once every 50 years) and for hazard class 2 the likelihood of a flood is set at 0.005 per year (once every 200 years). The flood risk for Baden-Wuerttemberg's roads in respect of indirect losses including external costs is depicted in Figure 40. A correlation between the flood risk and the criticality level of the links with regard to their short-term indirect loss potential cannot be observed. The main risk is on motorway A5 between Loerrach and Karlsruhe as well as close to Mannheim. Here the Rhine river poses the dominant threat. Other sections at risk are situated next to small rivers, streams or lakes, which often serve as feeders for the main rivers. The highest risk with ca. 108,000 Euro per year is bound to an A6 link south of Mannheim. The spending and actions for flood protection measures should be assessed in relation to these expected indirect losses and the expected other types of losses (e.g. direct losses), which are not estimated here.

[51] Based on the author's own investigations in Google Earth

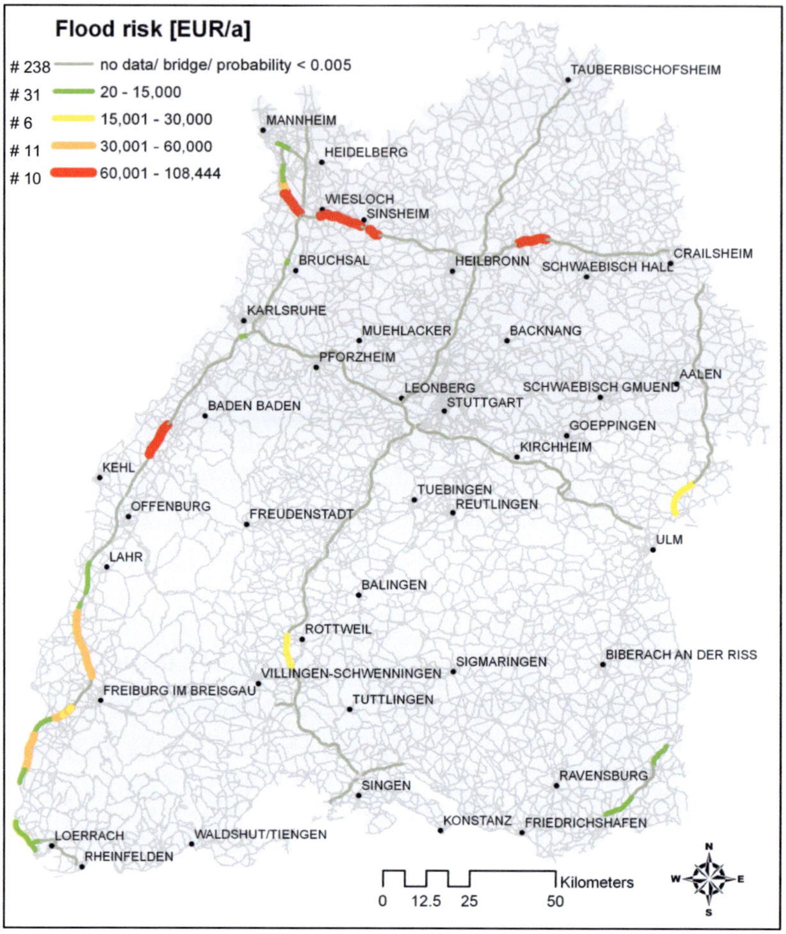

Figure 40: Flood risk on Baden-Wuerttemberg's motorways in respect of indirect losses in Euro per year

5.3 RECAPITULATION OF THE CASE STUDY'S RESULTS

This chapter presented the results of the Baden-Wuerttemberg case study. The most critical motorway links concentrate on the A8 south of Stuttgart. Including external costs, the short-term losses range from ca. 2,000 to 2,000,000 Euro per day. Excluding external costs, the short-term losses amount to 1,500 to 1,600,000 Euro per day and are reduced in the medium-term by ca. 10%, while the criticality ranking stays almost unaffected. According to the correlation analysis, the indirect losses are largely determined by the time costs, and also correlate to a medium extent with the (directly and indirectly) affected vehicles. Traffic counts, respectively the average daily number of vehicles on the affected road sections, turned out to be a reasonable approximation to the criticality ranking. On the other hand, the length of a road section showed no significant correlation with the ranking. The sensitivity analysis of the short-term losses with the alternative VOTnew revealed hardly any influence on the criticality ranking, especially on the ranking of the most critical links. This indicates that very short time delays due to a road section's closure rather pose an exception. Setting the results into the context of construction sites and the corresponding bonus/malus payments, there is a high discrepancy in terms of the short-term losses. This can be explained by the different degrees of assumed closure, but also by the derivation of the height of payments. So far, bonus/malus payments have nothing to do with the concept of short-term losses presented here, despite the associated underlying idea.

Arguing about potential indirect losses without any consideration of the probability of disruption makes it hard to identify countermeasures, and to justify spending on risk management measures. This chapter hence identified road sections of high indirect loss risk based on their susceptibility to failure (multi hazards) and indirect loss potential. The most critical links with regard to their indirect loss potential happen to be also the ones holding the highest level of susceptibility to failure and, consequently, the ones at highest indirect loss risk. Moreover, this chapter combined a flood hazard analysis and the calculated potential indirect losses to determine the expected indirect losses in a year caused by a one-day flood related closure – the indirect flood risk. The results range from zero to ca. 108,000 Euro. The most critical links based on indirect loss flood risk differ greatly from the ones based only on potential indirect losses. Further CI analyses should focus on the sections associated with high indirect loss risk.

6 BADEN-WUERTTEMBERG CASE STUDY: SIMULTANEOUS MULTIPLE ROAD CLOSURES

In the following sections, two scenarios of disrupted infrastructures due to natural events demonstrate the application of the loss calculation methodology to events of multiple failures. The first scenario is based on an earthquake that happened in 1911 in Ebingen, and demonstrates the effects if such an earthquake were to happen nowadays. The second scenario presents a flood in Esslingen with a return period of 200 years, which corresponds to a probability of 0.5% per year. The scenarios available for this study are restricted to non-motorways only. However, the principles of the proceedings are transferable to other types of disrupted roads.

In the context of multiple road failures, the VISMOD and VISEP tools, not available for this study, have to be mentioned. The tools adjust transportation networks for scenarios such as temporarily flooded areas, and calculate evacuation plans using the transport modeling software VISUM (Boden et al. (2007); Boden and Weger (2009)), which has also been used for the Baden-Wuerttemberg case study. The application of the tools to the two scenarios would most likely add interesting insights, especially in respect of disaster management, given that more data on other modes and modes' flows and networks are available. However, travel demand changes due to capacity degradations serve as external input in VISMOD. For example, Boden and Weger (2009) assume that the percentage of flooded areas in one traffic zone corresponds to the percentage of demand reduction. Also, there is, so far, no application to loss assessment or CI identification by the tools. In respect of destination choice changes and loss assessment, the calculation of the two scenarios in this chapter therefore poses a novelty.

6.1 SCENARIO: EARTHQUAKE IN EBINGEN

One of the biggest earthquakes Germany ever[52] experienced happened at 48°22' N and 9° E on 16th November 1911 at 21:25h, at a depth of 10km. This was below the city of Ebingen, south of Tuebingen (Grünthal and Wahlström (2003)). The local Richter magnitude amounted to M_L=6.1. In total, 6,250 buildings were damaged, resulting in a loss of ca. 120 million Eu-

[52] Included in historical records

ro[53] (Grünthal (2004); Münchner Rückversicherungs-Gesellschaft (1999), p.41). The Center for Disaster Management and Risk Reduction Technology (CEDIM)[54] modeled a simplified scenario of an earthquake happening nowadays with the same characteristics as that of 1911. Soil conditions and liquefaction were not considered due to a lack of data. The modeled intensities on the European Macroseismic Scale have a geographical distribution as depicted in Figure 41. The earthquake would be felt throughout the whole of Baden-Wuerttemberg. However, serious damage to buildings would only be expected in the close vicinity of the epicenter. A short description on the typically observed effects in the corresponding intensity zones is given in Table 18.

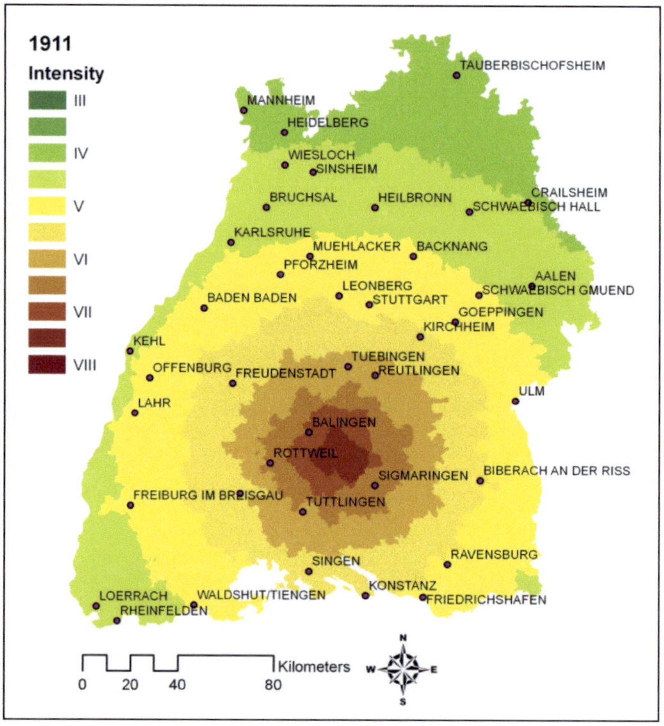

Figure 41: Intensity distribution following a 1911-like earthquake

[53] Prices in 2009

[54] Karlsruhe Institute of Technology (KIT), Institute of Reinforced Concrete Structures and Building Materials, Department of Reinforced Concrete Structures, scientist in charge of the scenario: Dr. Sergey Tyagunov

EMS intensity	Definition	Description of typical observed effects (abstracted)
I	Not felt	Not felt.
II	Scarcely felt	Felt only by very few individual people at rest in houses.
III	Weak	Felt indoors by a few people. People at rest feel a swaying or light trembling.
IV	Largely observed	Felt indoors by many people, outdoors by very few. A few people are awakened. Windows, doors and dishes rattle.
V	Strong	Felt indoors by most, outdoors by few. Many sleeping people awake. A few frightened. Buildings tremble throughout. Hanging objects swing considerably. Small objects are shifted. Doors and windows swing open or shut.
VI	Slightly damaging	Many people are frightened and run outdoors. Some objects fall. Many houses suffer slight non-structural damage like hair-line cracks and fall of small pieces off plaster
VII	Damaging	Most people are frightened and run outdoors. Furniture is shifted and objects fall from shelves in large number. Many well built ordinary buildings suffer moderate damage: small cracks in walls, fall of plaster, parts of chimneys fall down; older buildings may show large cracks in walls and failure of fill-in walls.
VIII	Heavily damaging	Many people find it difficult to stand. Many houses have large cracks in walls. A few well built ordinary buildings show serious failure of walls, while weak older structures may collapse.
IX	Destructive	General panic. Many weak constructions collapse. Even well built ordinary buildings show very heavy damage: serious failure of walls and partial structural failure.
X	Very destructive	Many ordinary well built buildings collapse.
XI	Devastating	Most ordinary well built buildings collapse, even some with good earthquake resistant design are destroyed.
XII	Completely devastating	Almost all buildings are destroyed.

Table 18: European Macroseismic Scale (EMS) intensity description (Grünthal (1998), p.99)

The impact of such an earthquake on the serviceability of roads depends on the condition of the artifacts along (e.g. buildings) or on/above/below such roads (e.g. a bridge). Probably a few street lights would collapse and parts of roof tops and chimneys would fall on selected roads. The pictures in Figure 42 visualize the expected seriousness of damage to residential buildings. Most buildings in the area of greatest intensity would experience damage corresponding to category 2[55] (left picture), while some would show category 3 damage (right picture).

[55] For more information on damage categories of certain housing types and earthquake intensities see Grünthal (1998).

Figure 42: Exemplified earthquake induced building damages of category 2 (left) (1978, Albstadt, Germany) and 3 (right) (1995, North Peloponnissos, Greece) (Grünthal (1998), p.73, p.77)

The direct losses to residential buildings in the scenario are estimated to amount to 1,225 million Euro (Tyagunov et al. (2006a)). However, the information on the degree of damage to residential houses does not allow deriving implications on the serviceability of roads. Other possible disruption causes are the failure of tunnels and bridges. Due to missing data on the soil conditions in the tunnels' surroundings, and hence a lack of information on the liquefaction potential of tunnels, possible damage and road disruption potential could not be considered in the scenario. Yet, for bridges, this is possible. The input parameters such as location, material, size, condition and type of bridge on main roads suffice for a simplified modeling (Tyagunov et al. (2007)). Generally applicable vulnerability and restoration time functions for German bridges are so far lacking[56]. Therefore, vulnerability functions developed in the U.S. for various bridge types (Applied Technology Council (ATC) (1991)), as well as the corresponding restoration time functions, serve as reference for the modeling of the expected bridge damage and duration of closure. Here, it was assumed that bridges in the area of 'California 7' are most similar to German construction practices. Consequently, only bridges within zones of intensity VIII need closer examination. Four bridges turn out to be at risk. While three of them may be inaccessible due to inspections for a duration lasting from a day up to one week, one bridge is likely to experience more serious damage leading to repairs taking up to a month. The road links 1 to 6 affected by these bridges are depicted in Figure 43. They are all part of the main B463 road. The flowbundles of the road links show that they are predomi-

[56] Meskouris et al. (2007) developed vulnerability functions for three specific bridges in Germany. The portability of the specific functions for the application on other bridges is very restricted.

nantly used as east-west connection in southern Baden-Wuerttemberg, between the Black Forest and the Swabian Alb (see Figure 44 and Figure 45). For simplification purposes, it was assumed that the road links would be completely disrupted after the event. In reality, it might be possible that only one lane is closed and the remaining lane is shared in both directions with traffic light signaling. Depending on the duration of the red light phase, and the corresponding expected travel time, some users might still choose to make a detour or decide on another destination. It is therefore reasonable to assume that the closure scenario here is rather strict, and is consequently more costly than with a less strict assumption. According to the expected direct losses to buildings, some local roads may also be blocked due to debris or other obstacles, and may therefore fail as routing alternatives. It is assumed that these types of blockage are of an insignificant extent, and are therefore ignored.

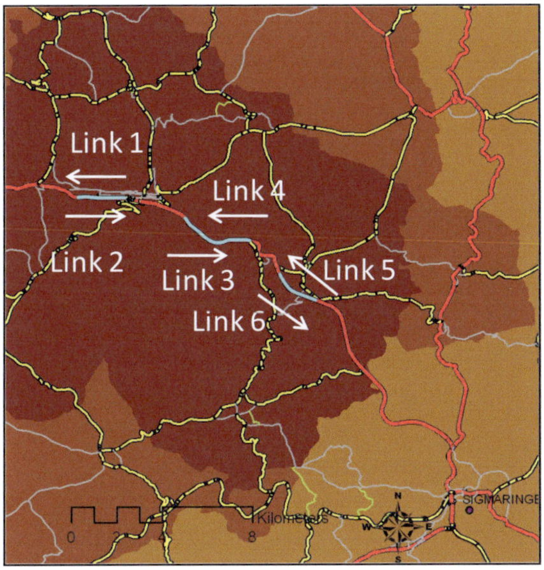

Figure 43: The Ebingen earthquake scenario with affected links due to bridge closure

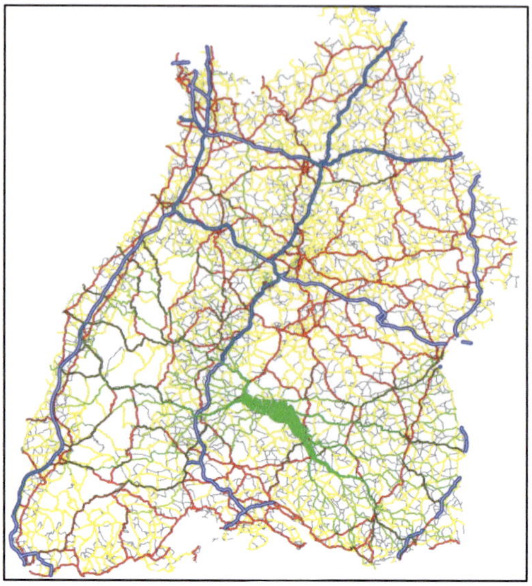

Figure 44: Truck flowbundle (green) of the Ebingen earthquake scenario's affected links

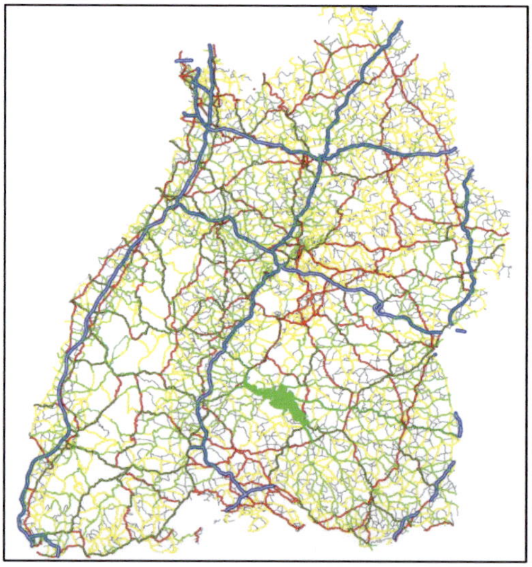

Figure 45: Passenger car flowbundle (green) of the Ebingen earthquake scenario's affected links

The damage degree for the modeled intensity retrieved from the vulnerability functions provided by the Applied Technology Council (ATC) (1991) (p.202ff), combined with the size of the bridge and the average monetary values of certain bridge types (Hinsch et al. (2001); Rommerskirchen et al. (2009)), allows an estimation of the direct costs of the bridge failure in the earthquake scenario. Assuming a 10% damage to the most affected and a 0-2% damage to the least affected bridges according to the American vulnerability functions, the direct losses would amount to ca. 190,000 Euro[57].

The (first order) indirect losses due to the bridge closures are summarized in Figure 46. They are based on the methodology and assumptions outlined in Chapter 3. The physically less affected bridges are assumed to be closed for one week, and the more affected bridge for a month. The losses are displayed on a per day basis and as a sum of the respective period. In the first three days the losses amount to ca. 141,000 Euro including external costs when applying the VOTold. With the VOTnew losses are reduced to ca. 130,000 Euro. They contain the short-term losses entailed by re-routing the six disrupted road sections. The usage of the VOTnew therefore reduces the short term losses based on the VOTold by 8%. This reduction results from detours which are shorter than an average of 5 minutes.

From the fourth day onwards the indirect costs per day decline, following adjusted destination choices and the reopening of links 3 to 6 after a week. For the rest of the duration of the closure, the medium-term losses caused by the disrupted links 1 and 2 are taken into account. Overall, the indirect losses add up to ca. 518,000 Euro including external costs. The average daily first-order indirect losses are ca. 17,000 Euro.

[57] Meantime, the link with the highest damage potential became profoundly retrofitted in 2010 (Much (2010)) but had been in worse condition when the study was made.

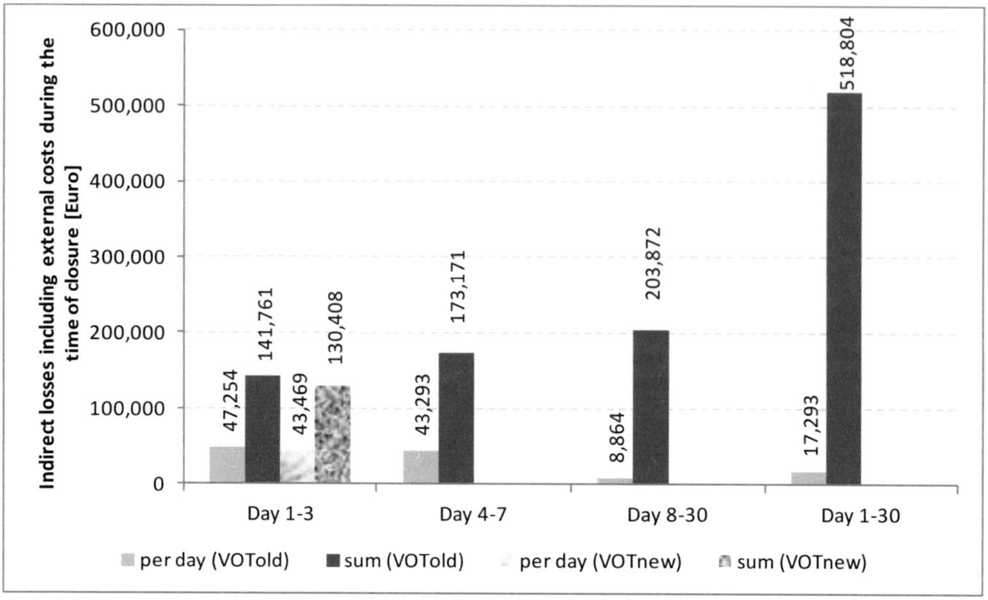

Figure 46: Indirect losses in the Ebingen earthquake scenario due to bridge closure

The ratio between direct and indirect costs caused by the damaged bridges is 35%, meaning that the indirect costs dominate the direct costs by ca. two thirds. However, compared to the direct costs caused by the damaged houses, the bridge induced losses become marginal (0.06%).

A criticality study of the individual road links points out the ones whose serviceability should be restored first. Setting the individual capacity of the affected road links in the scenario to zero entails short- and medium-term indirect losses as depicted in Figure 47. The two bridges connected with road links 3 and 4 pose the highest indirect loss potential, and should therefore receive a higher priority in refitting. Another interesting insight of Figure 47 is that the most critical links show the highest indirect loss reduction potential due to destination choice changes (8-9%), while the links with low indirect losses obviously have attractive rerouting possibilities. Using the VOTnew reduces the indirect losses related to each road section's closure by ca. 5-30%. Consequently many, of the respective detours are shorter than 5 minutes.

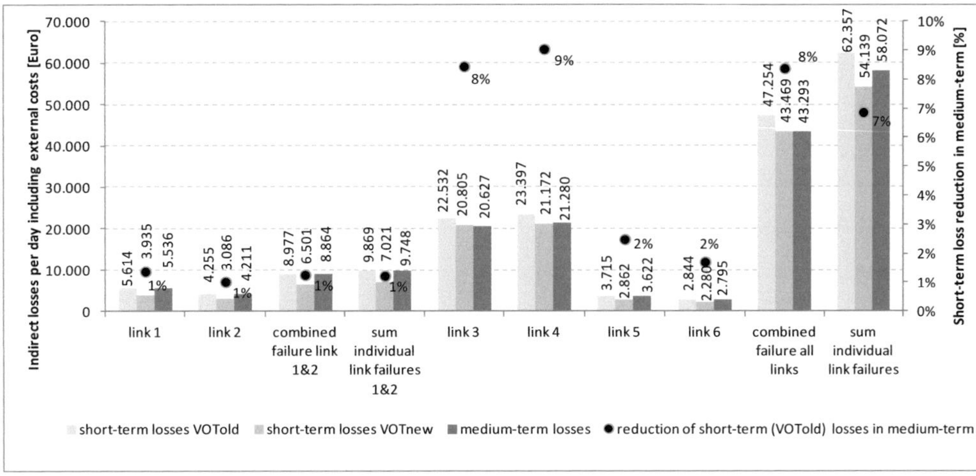

Figure 47: Short- and medium-term indirect losses in the Ebingen earthquake scenario due to bridge closure including external costs

Figure 47 also reveals that the sum of the indirect losses of the individual links' closure exceeds the indirect losses of the combined failure by ca. 15,000 Euro, which corresponds to ca. 30%. This also means that the indirect losses, and hence the place in the criticality ranking of the links, is rather overestimated in the event that they fail together. This holds for all six links together, but to a minor degree also for links 1 and 2. According to the definitions given earlier, this indicates a complementarity of the links. It is, however, surprising that links 1 and 2 are not strictly additive in their losses, since they are reverse links to each other. The slight complementary effect can be explained by the synchronic usage of specific road sections on the detours of affected vehicles and on the 'normal' route of the non-affected vehicles.

It has to be mentioned that the utilized transport model (the combination of VALIDATE and the logit model) was calibrated to predominantly match the motorway traffic counts and serve for the main purpose of this study. Focusing on a rural area like that surrounding Ebingen or Esslingen (in the following scenario) with many minor roads would have required a different calibration of the model. While the traffic counts on the affected road links in the area of Ebingen match to an acceptable level the estimated traffic on links 3 to 6, traffic on links 1 and 2 is underestimated (-50%) (in comparison to Straßenbauverwaltung Baden-Württemberg (2007), southern part). This can be interpreted as confirmation that there are attractive rerouting alternatives for links 1 and 2. Thus it also shows that the criticality analysis and the connected indirect loss estimation would probably differ in a model with a better fit. For indirect loss assessments in small case study areas, the application of a transport model which is well calibrated for this area is recommended. If this is not available, it is at least advisable to compare any hints on result-distorting influences, as has been done in this case.

6.2 Scenario: Flood in Esslingen

The cities along the river Neckar have already undergone many floods[58]. Dikes, wears and retention basins were able to protect the cities from devastation and major losses in the last few decades. However, some flood measures are likely to fail in the event of an infrequent strong flooding event. The scope of this scenario is a flood with a 200 year return period in the city of Esslingen, ca. 10 km southeast of Stuttgart, and in particular the district of Sirnau. The scenario is based on a study of the Institut für Wasser und Gewässerentwicklung at the Karlsruhe Institute of Technology (KIT) (Institut für Wasser und Gewässerentwicklung (2005)). According to the study, the dikes are expected to be breached and therefore fail as protection for the hydraulically connected zone. Consequently the whole district (ca. 1 km²), including the main, district and local roads, is flooded (see the red lined area in Figure 48) for an assumed duration of two days.

Figure 48: Flooded area in a 200 year event in Sirnau (own illustration in Google Earth based on Institut für Wasser und Gewässerentwicklung (2005))

[58] A list of historical events is given in IKoNE (2006), Appendix 2.

In 2005[59], Sirnau had 827 inhabitants with around 75% of potential employees between 15 and 65 years of age, ca. 12% children below the age of 15 and 13% elderly people above 65 years[60]. One part of the district is a living area with ca. 375 living units. The other part is an industrial area with a wholesale market, a hardware store, a bus operator, a firm producing construction chemicals and some others. The relevant roads are of high importance to the inhabitants and to the local companies, since they offer the only access to their homes and work, and they are also used by commuters and freight companies heading further north to a large automotive manufacturer. It is a main connection between the city of Stuttgart, Esslingen and the city of Goeppingen (east of Esslingen). Apart from the interrupted road infrastructure and the consequent triggered effects, the following flood related occurrences influencing direct and indirect overall losses are expected:

- The inhabitants and companies of Sirnau receive an early warning with regard to the expected event through media or public authorities (e.g. Baden Wuerttemberg's flood warning centre[61]). They even have time to bring some of their belongings into shelter before evacuation measures are taken. Assuming a two day flood, the clean-up and repairs probably take days to months.
- During the flood and clean up phase, the working inhabitants (max. 620) do most likely not go to work. As long as they do not all share the same employer, their absence in the work place, and the corresponding loss of output, does not significantly contribute to the indirect losses.
- The companies in the flooded area of Sirnau have to shut down during the flood and potentially during the clean up phase. Customers and employees have difficulties in reaching them. Direct damage by the flood could trigger interruptions for suppliers and customers throughout the whole supply chain.
- The dwellings' assets, exposed to the flood, amount to 43-65 million Euro[62]. It is unlikely that all buildings and their contents lose their complete value in the course of the flood. Therefore the 43-65 million Euro can be considered as the absolute maximum direct damage to dwellings in Sirnau.

[59] In conformity with the data base of the indirect loss estimation model
[60] Based on the city's homepage: http://www.esslingen.de/servlet/PB/menu/1333030_l1/index.html [1.2.2011]
[61] http://www.hvz.baden-wuerttemberg.de/
[62] Source: Sirnau's number of inhabitants multiplied by dwelling assets per inhabitant in the area of Esslingen retrieved from Cedim Risk Explorer http://cedim.gfz-potsdam.de/riskexplorer/ [1.2.2011] converted to prices in 2005. The methodology behind the asset estimation is described in Thieken et al. (2006) and Kleist et al. (2006).

- The exposed industrial assets are estimated on the basis of Seifert et al. (2010) converted to prices in 2005. Close to Stuttgart there is an average asset value per m² of 172 Euro in respect of manufacturing companies. Assuming similar values for Sirnau's industrial area, which covers about one third of Sirnau, the flood results in a maximum of 57 million Euro direct losses.

Direct damage to the roads is hard to predict since there are no vulnerability functions available. A maximum damage level 5 (see Table 3 in Chapter 2.2.1) with serious damage to all road layers, and with a necessary renewal of the whole road in the complete district of Sirnau, corresponds to maximal costs of 40-50 million Euro for earthworks (including planning) and superstructure (base, binder and road surface). The calculations are based on Rommerskirchen et al. (2009) (p.74ff) and their cost estimations for the construction of new German supraregional roads (main roads and motorways). Of course, not all roads are likely to be completely destroyed, and district roads and smaller roads inside the village are cheaper than motorways and main roads. Consequently, the range of direct road costs are at the very maximum, which can be expected.

Depending on the seriousness of the damage, the roads might be usable immediately after the flood has retreated and having been cleaned up, which corresponds to a loss of serviceability of 3 days up to possibly a week (assuming the flood lasting 2 days). In the event of a maximum damage level and all roads needing to be rebuilt, the interruption might take months, although it is realistic that access to companies and houses is quickly restored with provisional measures. During the flood, many trips are likely to be suppressed, a situation which cannot be captured with the available data and the model developed for this study. Since the injection of traffic born in the traffic zone of Sirnau also has an injection point outside the flooded area, the origin/destination still exists, and no trips have to be suppressed. The indirect costs due to a three day closure of all roads (VALIDATE's network only contains the main and district roads in this area) amount to 1.02 million Euro respectively 1.08 million Euro when the 'new' VOT is used. In this case the 'new' VOT increases the losses by ca. 5% as short detours are apparently rare. A month of interruption entails indirect losses of ca. 10 million Euro (see Figure 49).

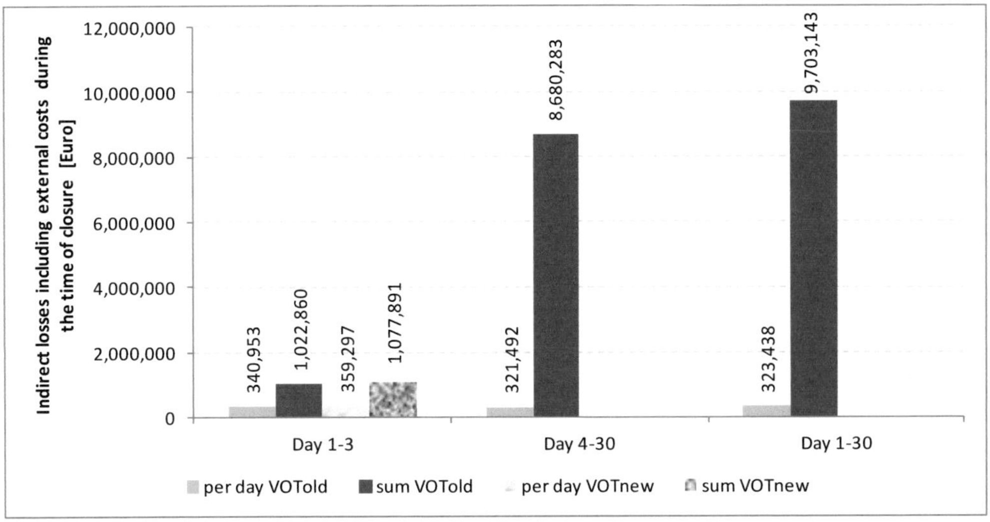

Figure 49: Indirect losses in the flood scenario due to road closures

The maximum direct road related losses amount to ca. 40-50 million Euro. A month of interruption is therefore as costly as 20-25% of the maximum direct road-related losses. However, it is likely that the costs of damaged dwellings, industry area and equipment (max. ca. 100 million Euro) exceed the direct and indirect losses associated with the road closure.

Figure 51 shows the short- and medium-term losses in the event of single and multiple failures. The corresponding links are displayed in Figure 50. Link 9 turns out to be the most critical one in addition to links 10, 1 and 2. They are all main roads and carry more vehicles than the district or local roads (links 3 to 8). The multiple link failure displays the complementarity of the link set. The deviation from additivity is ca. 10%, which suggests a slight complementarity in terms of the links. Looking at the link set, substitutability would actually be expected. This is confirmed when closing links 2 and 4 simultaneously which entails ca. 84,000 Euro indirect losses. In comparison, their individual disruption results in a sum of ca. 52,000 Euro losses (not displayed in the Figures). The complementarity of the other links in the set however overlaps and exceeds the substitutional effects. For links 2 and 4, the indirect losses, and hence the criticality, is rather underestimated in the event of a combined failure. But the whole set of links affected by the flood shows a trend of overestimation in terms of indirect losses and criticality.

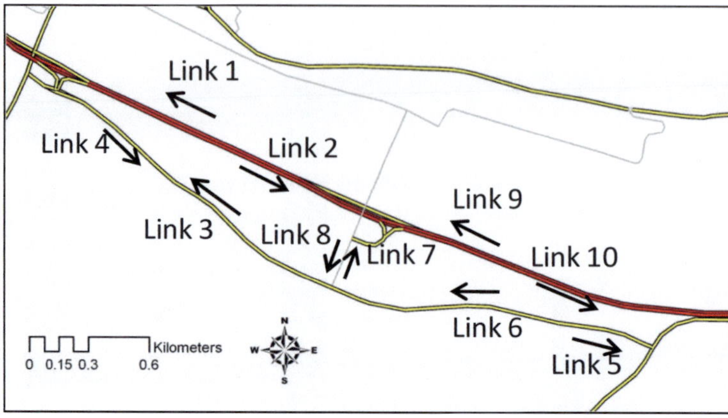

Figure 50: The Esslingen flood scenario's affected links

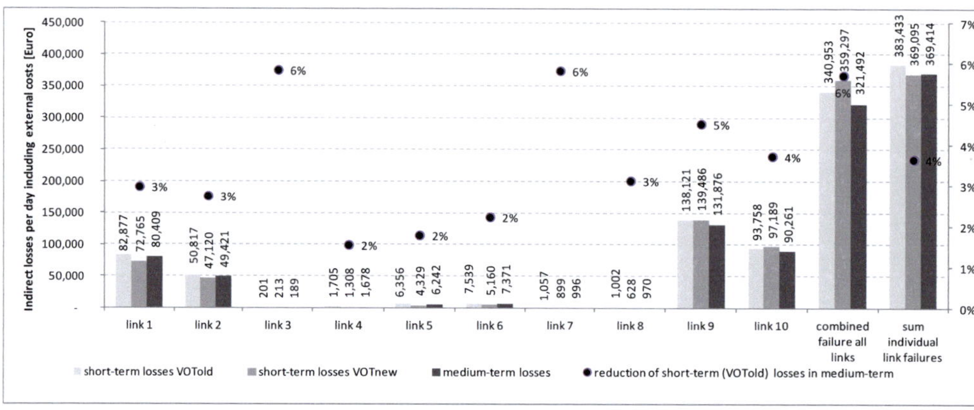

Figure 51: Short- and medium-term indirect losses in the flood scenario due to road closures including external costs

The application of the VOTnew shows varying effects depending on the road section. While the indirect losses related to the closures of links 3, 9 and 10 increase, the losses caused by the interruption of links 1, 2 and 4 to 8 are smaller than with the VOTold. This means that the closure of these latter links provoke predominantly detours taking less than 5 minutes.

In contrast to the results of the earthquake scenario, here the links with the highest indirect loss reduction potential in the medium-term, links 3 and 7, do not correspond to the links with the highest short-term indirect losses, links 9 and 10. This is consistent with the findings of the correlation analysis of the short-term losses and the medium-term loss reduction potential associated with the motorway links in the Baden-Wuerttemberg case study (see Table 13 in Chapter 5.1.1).

6.3 RECAPITULATION OF THE SCENARIOS WITH SIMULTANEOUS MULTIPLE ROAD CLOSURES

The case of simultaneous failure of multiple infrastructures has so far hardly found attention in current research on the identification of CIs. However, in realistic, serious disruption scenarios, more than just one infrastructure is likely to be affected. Geographical or other interdependencies may interrupt multiple road infrastructure sections and other infrastructure sectors such as energy, telecommunication, railways, etc. The combination of affected infrastructures may amplify or attenuate the indirect losses as described in section 3.4. This chapter exemplified the emergence of these effects in the presented scenarios of an earthquake and a flood-related event. In both cases the combined failure entailed less indirect losses than the sum of losses caused by individual failures. This indicates a complementarity of the link set, and therefore a tendency to overestimate the criticality of the links in such scenarios.

In the earthquake scenario, set in a rural area, indirect losses of ca. 500,000 Euro for a month occurred, while in the flood scenario in the vicinity of Stuttgart, the indirect losses amounted to 10 million Euro for the same period. The comparison of the indirect losses with the estimated direct losses in the scenarios underlined the significant part physical damage plays in the overall cost, depending on the assumed seriousness of the damage.

7 SUMMARY AND FUTURE CHALLENGES

7.1 SUMMARY

In the past decades the necessity to protect CIs has increasingly found supporters in politics and society, and has aroused the interest of researchers with manifold backgrounds. Not least because of the terror attacks in New York, Madrid and London as well as the recent events in Japan, the need to even consider unthinkable incidents and to identify hot spots in society's lifelines has become an urgent topic on political agendas. National and international activities like the European Directive 2008/114/EC "on the Identification and Designation of European Critical Infrastructure (ECI) and the Assessment of the Need to Improve their Protection" mark elementary steps towards a greater awareness of possible societal risks due to lifeline disruptions. The transportation sector with its road network as one of the CIs accounted for in the agendas was a focus of this thesis.

Many challenges have emerged with the identification of CIs and the implementation of the Directive and other guidelines. First of all, there are various involved parties such as private operators, the Ministry of the Interior, Defense and/or Transport as well as the European Commission which makes communication, the allocation of competencies and data exchange (often confidential), a rather complicated undertaking. Secondly, the requirements, such as in the Directive, tend to be fairly unspecific, especially in respect to the threshold above which an infrastructure may be considered as critical. Though the mentioned criteria in the Directive, casualties, economic and public effects, define what type of consequences shall be included in the assessment, public hints on how these consequences shall be measured or calculated are missing. This opens up room for further research activities.

Research projects carried out by miscellaneous disciplines already contribute to the identification of hot spots in lifelines, predominantly based on indices. The estimation of economic effects caused by lifeline disruptions is often performed by input-output models. Estimating the effects of a road infrastructure disruption on trip making behaviour usually requires a transport model. A logit-based approach therein provides the option to even monetize changes in trip making decisions such as destination or modal choice. This thesis built on such a concept as a means of assessing economic (first-order) indirect costs due to road disruptions, and ranked the road links according to their indirect loss potential. Indirect costs refer to the loss of serviceability of a road section and the immediate effects on road users. The thesis suggested a monetized loss calculation methodology with a single measure that captures changes on various trip making decision levels, and accounts for the duration of disruption. The further suggested systematization of the effects of multiple road sections' failures allows a reinterpretation of the criticality assessment, depending on the combination of affected links. A standardized transportation infrastructure criticality assessment could use the suggested insights and methodology as a basis for more detailed analyses of the most critical sections.

The methodology was applied to the study area of Baden-Wuerttemberg and its motorway network. The results revealed the magnitude of expected indirect losses due to complete single road section closure, with variations between the examined road sections (ca. 0.002 to 2 million Euro) leading to a more or less critical account. Time costs turned out to be the determining indirect loss driver. The criticality ranking of the short-term losses correlates moderately with the ranking based on the average daily number of vehicles on the affected road section. Thus the commonly available average daily traffic values may serve as first approximation for critical road sections.

In order to justify spending on risk management measures, a monetization of losses and knowledge of the probability of failure are crucial. The thesis combined the indirect losses with a qualitative measure of susceptibility of failure and also with quantitative probabilities of flooding. It demonstrated the (indirect loss) risk levels of the road sections under consideration, and revealed that the most critical links based on the indirect loss ranking are not necessarily the links with the highest indirect loss risks.

The two road disrupting scenarios of an earthquake and a flood in Baden-Wuerttemberg demonstrated the application of the indirect loss calculation methodology in the context of multiple simultaneous failures, and set the indirect losses in relation to estimated direct losses. Depending on the seriousness of physical damage, indirect losses turned out to be only marginal compared to direct losses. Even if their contribution to the overall losses might be negligible in certain situations, their assessment might still be valuable for reconstruction decisions.

Therefore, the thesis at hand has contributed significantly to answering important issues in respect of CI identification and indirect loss calculation methodology. It may assist practitioners or politicians in the design and implementation process of national or international CI programs. Nevertheless, some further questions are still left to be considered.

7.2 Future challenges

Realistic failures of CIs are not bound to a total loss of serviceability. This is, however, a common modeling basis for the identification of CIs (see, for example, Jenelius et al. (2006); Nagurney and Qiang (2008); Erath (2010)). Accordingly, it was assumed in this thesis. The methodology suggested here also allows for less strict capacity reductions. Future works could analyze the effects on the criticality ranking under a new capacity constraint assumption.

Another aspect, not sufficiently studied so far, are dynamic changes in trip making behavior due to, for example, dynamic updates in information, disaster management activities or changes in infrastructure condition. Organizational measures like the temporary reallocation of one of the lanes in the other direction might help to reduce the indirect losses in the medium-term. Further research is required to understand the influences on trip making behavior immediately after an incident, and later to improve transport modeling in unusual circumstances, and hence to assist, for example, decision-makers in emergency management. At the same time, a better integration of the research activities of different disciplines (e.g. economics, psychology, engineering, etc.) and authorities (e.g. universities, civil protection...) is inevitable.

This thesis made a cut at the indirect first order effects. Closely connected to affected freight transportation are the logistic processes behind them. Depending on the severity of the upper order effects (direct and first order indirect effects), serious problems with regard to the supply of necessary goods may occur. Platz (2005)[63], for example, analyses the effects of disturbing events on the logistics of the food trade sector and hence on society's food supply. The ongoing project, RM-LOG[64], sponsored by the Bundesministerium für Bildung und Forschung in Germany, explores various disrupting scenarios and their impact on supply chains. It further identifies adequate risk management strategies for companies and public authorities in order to secure the supply of goods. A combination of the methodology and the findings of this thesis with the studies on the effects of logistic systems may contribute to a better understanding of the emergence of indirect losses.

Lacking more detailed data, the thesis applied a pragmatic approach in order to obtain a transport model capable of fulfilling the requirements of the study's objectives. Surely, more

[63] A short version in English can be found in Platz (2007).
[64] More information on the project can be found at: www.rmlog.de [16.03.2011].

data and efforts would lead to a more precise modeling basis. However, the main focus of this thesis was to demonstrate the indirect loss modeling technique in the context of CI identification, rather than demonstrating up to date transport modeling methodologies. Further information on the estimation of transport models can be found in the relevant literature.

Scarce time and resources often prevent decision-makers in politics or companies from applying recommended procedures, here the identification of CIs. The thesis showed that a rough assessment of road sections' criticality, performed using traffic count data, generated results correlating with the outcome of the more complex indirect loss calculations. It is, nevertheless, essential to analyze the most important links in respect of potential disrupting causes, simultaneously affected infrastructures, as well as detouring possibilities, in more detail. In order to justify expenditures on risk management measures, an estimation of expected monetized losses can hardly be avoided.

REFERENCES

Albert, R. and Barabási, A.-L. (2002). Statistical mechanics of complex networks. In: *Reviews of Modern Physics*. 74. 47-97.

AMR and HCG (1996). *The value of travel time on UK roads - 1994*. Report. Accent Marketing Research and Hague Consulting Group prepared for the Department of Transport: The Hague.

Applied Technology Council (ATC) (1991). *Seismic vulnerability and impact of disruption of lifelines in the conterminous United States (ATC-25)*. Earthquake Hazard Reduction Series 58. ATC: Redwood City, California.

Arbeitsgruppe Verkehrsplanung (1997). *Empfehlungen für Wirtschaftlichkeitsuntersuchungen an Straßen (EWS) - Aktualisierung der RAS-W 86*. Draft Issue 1997. Forschungsgesellschaft für Strassen- und Verkehrswesen, Arbeitsgruppe Verkehrsplanung: Köln.

BABS (2010). *Schlussbericht Kritikalität der Teilsektoren - Programm Schutz Kritischer Infrastrukturen*. Final Report prepared for the Schweizerische Bundesrat. 11.9.2010. Bundesamt für Bevölkerungsschutz BABS, Schweizerische Eidgenossenschaft: Bern.

Bates, J. and Whelan, G. (2001). Size and sign of travel time savings. In: *ITS Working Papers*. 561.

Beer, T. and Ziolkowski, F. (1995). *Environmental risk assessment: An Australian perspective*. Supervising Scientist Report Number 102. Commonwealth of Australia.

Ben-Akiva, M. E. and Bowman, J. L. (1998). Activity based travel demand model systems. In: *Equilibrium and advanced transportation modelling*. Marcotte, P. and Ngyen, S. (Eds.). Kluwer Academic Publishers: Boston/ Dordrecht/ London. 27-46.

Ben-Akiva, M. E. and Lerman, S. R. (1985). *Discrete choice analysis: theory and application to travel demand*. MIT Press: Cambridge, Massachusetts.

Berdica, K. (2002). An introduction to road vulnerability: what has been done, is done and should be done. In: *Transport Policy*. 9. 117-127.

Berdica, K. and Eliasson, J. (2004). Regional accessibility analysis from a vulnerability perspective. In: *Proceedings of the Second International Symposium on Transportation Network Reliability*. 20.-24.08.2004 in Christchurch and Queenstown, New Zealand. 89-94.

Birkmann, J. (2007). Risk and vulnerability indicators at different scales: Applicability, usefulness and policy implications. In: *Environmental Hazards*. 7. 20-31.

Birn, K., Bolik, H. and Rieken, P. (2005). *Die gesamtwirtschaftliche Bewertungsmethodik - Bundesverkehrswegeplan 2003*. Final Report, FE-Nr. 70.0736/2003. Bundesministerium für Verkehr, Bau- und Wohnungswesen: Bonn/Berlin.

BMI (2007). *Schutz kritischer Infrastrukturen - Risiko- und Krisenmanagement: Leitfaden für Unternehmen und Behörden*. Brochure. Bundesministerium des Innern: Berlin.

BMI (2009a). *National Strategy for Critical Infrastructure Protection*. Brochure. Bundesministerium des Innern: Berlin.

BMI (2009b). *National Strategy for Critical Infrastructure Protection (CIP Strategy)*. Brochure. Bundesministerium des Innern: Berlin.

BMVBS (2010a). *Handbuch für die Vergabe und Ausführung von Bauleistungen im Straßen- und Brückenbau - HVA B-StB*. Bundesministerium für Verkehr, Bau und Stadtentwicklung: Bonn.

BMVBS (2010b). *Summary of the cost benefit assessment parameters of all road projects in the 'BVWP 2003'*. Internal data file. Bundesministerium für Verkehr, Bau und Stadtentwicklung (BMVBS): Berlin

Boden, M., Buzna, L. and Weger, H. (2007). Simulation of evacuation scenarios in urban areas - developing tools for modeling and optimization of evacuation traffic flows. In: *TRANSCOM 2007: 7th European Conference of Young Researchers and Science Workers. Sect.1: Transport and communications technologies*. Žilinska Univerzita: Žilina.

Boden, M. and Weger, H. (2009). Entwicklung von Tools für eine effizientere Verkehrsmodellierung in makroskopischen Verkehrsnetzen. In: *Proceedings of the 22.Verkehrswissenschaftliche Tage*. 28.-29.9.2009 in Dresden, Germany.

Bol, G. (2004a). *Deskriptive Statistik*. Oldenbourg Wissenschaftsverlag: Munich.

Bol, G. (2004b). *Wahrscheinlichkeitstheorie*. Oldenbourg Wissenschaftsverlag: Munich.

Brookshire, D. S., Chang, S. E., Cochrane, H., Olson, R. A., Rose, A. and Steenson, J. (1997). Direct and Indirect Economic Losses from Earthquake Damage. In: *Earthquake Spectra*. 13 (4). 683-701.

Büchele, B., Kreibich, H., Kron, A., Thieken, A. H., Ihringer, J., Oberle, P., Merz, B. and Nestmann, F. (2006). Flood-risk mapping: contributions towards an enhanced assessment of extreme events and associated risks. In: *Natural Hazards and Earth System Sciences*. 6. 485-503.

Bush, B. B., Dauelsberg, L., LeClaire, R. J., Powell, D. R., DeLand, S. M. and Samsa, M. E. (2005). Critical Infrastructure Protection Decision Support System (CIP/DSS) Project Overview. In: *Conference Proceedings of the 23rd International Conference of the System Dynamics Society*. System Dynamics Society: Albany, NY. Paper No. 332.

BVU, ITP and planco (2009). *Aktualisierung von Bewertungsansätzen für Wirtschaftlichkeitsuntersuchungen in der Bundesverkehrswegeplanung*. Final report, November 2009. BVU, ITP and planco for Bundesministerium für Verkehr, Bau und Stadtentwicklung: Essen, Freiburg, München.

Cairns, S., Atkins, S. and Goodwin, P. (2002). Disappearing traffic? The story so far. In: *Municipal Engineer*. 151 (1). 13-22.

Cardellini, V., Casalicchio, E. and Galli, E. (2007). Agent-based modeling of interdependencies in critical infrastructures through UML. In: *SpringSim '07, Proceedings of the 2007 spring simulation multiconference*. Society for Computer simulation International: San Diego. Volume 2. 119-126.

Carreno, M.-L., Cardona, O. D. and Barbat, A. H. (2007). Urban Seismic Risk Evaluation: A Holistic Approach. In: *Natural Hazards*. 40. 137-172.

Chen, A., Yang, C., Kongsomsaksakul, S. and Lee, M. (2007). Network-based accessability measures for vulnerability analysis of degradable transportation networks. In: *Networks and Spatial Economics*. 7. 241-256.

Cho, S., Gordon, P., Moore, J. E. I., Richardson, H. W., Shinozuka, M. and Chang, S. E. (2001). Integrating transportation network and regional economic models to estimate the costs of a large urban earthquake. In: *Journal of Regional Science*. 41 (1). 39-65.

Cho, S., Gordon, P., Richardson, H. W., Moore, J. E. I. and Shinozuka, M. (2000). Analyzing transportation reconstruction network strategies: a full cost approach. In: *The Applied Regional Science Conference*. 12 (3). 212-227.

Cleff, T. (2008). *Deskriptive Statistik und moderne Datenanalyse - Eine computergestützte Einführung mit Excel, SPSS und STATA*. Gabler: Wiesbaden.

Cochrane, H. (2004). Economic loss: myth and measurement. In: *Disaster Prevention and Management*. 13 (4). 290-296.

Commission of the European Communities (2005). *Green Paper on a European Programme for Critical Infrastructure Protection*. COM(2005) 576 final.

Commission of the European Communities (2006a). *Communication from the Commission on a European Programme for Critical Infrastructure Protection*. COM(2006) 786 final.

Commission of the European Communities (2006b). *Proposal for a Directive of the Council on the identification and designation of European Critical Infrastructure and the assessment of the need to improve their protection*. COM(2006) 787 final, 2006/0276 (CNS).

Commonwealth Department of Health and Aged Care (DHAC) (2001). Measuring Remoteness: Accessability/Remoteness Index of Australia (ARIA). In: *Occasional Papers: New Series 14*. October 2001. Commonwealth Department of Health and Aged Care (DHAC): Canberra.

Council of the European Union (2008). *Directive on the identification and designation of European critical infrastructures and the assessment of the need to improve their protection*. Directive 2008/114/EG.

Dauelsberg, L. and Outkin, A. (2005). Critical Infrastructure Protection Decision Support. In: *Conference Proceedings of the 23rd International Conference of the System Dynamics Society*. System Dynamics Society: Albany, NY. Paper No. 278.

de Jong, G. (2008). Value of freight travel-time savings. In: *Handbook of transport modelling*. Hensher, D. A. and Button, K. J. (Eds.). Elsevier Science: Oxford. 649-663.

de Jong, G., Daly, A., Pieters, M. and van der Hoorn, T. (2005). The logsum as an evaluation measure: review of the literature and new results. In: *Proceedings of the 45th Congress of the European Regional Science Association*. 23.-27.08.2005 in Amsterdam.

de Jong, G., Daly, A., Pieters, M. and van der Hoorn, T. (2007). The logsum as an evaluation measure: Review of the literature and new results. In: *Transportation Research Part A*. 41. 874-889.

Deutsches Bundesamt für Sicherheit in der Informationstechnik (2004). *Analysis of Critical Infrastructures - The ACIS methodology*. Brochure. http://www.bsi.de/english/topics/kritis/acis_paper_en.pdf [10.4.2007].

Deutsches Institut für Wirtschaftsforschung (2010). *Verkehr in Zahlen 2009/2010*. Bundesministerium für Verkehr, Bau und Stadtentwicklung (eds.). Deutscher Verkehrs-Verlag: Hamburg.

ECLAC (2003). *Handbook for estimating the socio-economic and environmental effects of disasters*. United Nations Economic Commission for Latin America and the Carribean (ECLAC) and International Bank for Reconstruction and Development (The World Bank): Santiago, Chile.

Ellson, R. W., Milliman, J. W. and Roberts, R. B. (1984). Measuring the regional economic effects of earthquakes and earthquake predictions. In: *Journal of Regional Science*. 24 (4). 559-579.

Erath, A. (2010). Assessing network vulnerability using the CBA and logsum measure. In: *Proceedings of the 12th WCTR 2010*. 11.-15.7.2010 in Lisbon, Portugal.

Erath, A., Birdsall, J. D., Axhausen, K. W. and Hajdin, R. (2009). Vulnerability assessment methodology for Swiss Road Network. In: *Transportation Research Record: Journal of the Transportation Research Board*. 2137. 118-126.

Erdik, M. and Fahjan, Y. (2006). Damage scenarios and damage evaluation. In: *Assessing and Managing Earthquake Risk: Geo-scientific and Engineering Knowledge for Earthquake Risk Mitigation: developments, tools, techniques*. Oliveira, C. S., Roca, A. and Goula, X. (Eds.). Springer: Dordrecht. 228-231.

European Commission (2010). *Risk Assessment and Mapping Guidelines for Disaster Management*. Commission Staff Working Paper. SEC(2010) 1626 final. 21.12.2010. European Commission: Brussels.

European Environment Agency (2004). *Impacts of Europe's changing climate*. Report Number 2/2004. European Environment Agency: Copenhagen.

Eurostat (2010). *Energy prices - monthly data for the year 2005*. http://epp.eurostat.ec.europa.eu [24.3.2010].

Fritzon, A., Ljungkvist, K., Boin, A. and Rhinard, M. (2007). Protecting Europe's Critical Infrastructures: Problems and Prospects. In: *Journal of Contingencies and Crisis Management*. 15 (1). 30-41.

Garatwa, W. and Bollin, C. (2002). *Disaster Risk Management - Working Concept.* Brochure. Deutsche Gesellschaft für Technische Zusammenarbeit (GTZ): Eschborn.

GDV (2008). *Geo-Informationssystem "ZÜRS Geo": Zonierungssystem für Überschwemmungsrisiko und Einschätzung von Umweltrisiken.* Brochure. Gesamtverband der Deutschen Versicherungswirtschaft e.V.(GDV). www.gdv.de/Themen/Schadensverhuetung/NaturgewaltenElementarschaeden/inhaltsseite22828.html [9.3.2011].

Goll, U. (20.7.2010). *Vorsicht Hitzeschäden! Ackerfurchen in der Autobahn.* schwarzwaelder-bote.de. 20.7.2010. Schwarzwälder Bote Mediengesellschaft mbH: Oberndorf am Neckar. http://www.schwarzwaelder-bote.de/inhalt.vorsicht-hitzeschaeden-ackerfurchen-in-der-autobahn.956781fb-6028-4908-86c1-437f279d258e.html [3.9.2010].

Goodwin, P. B. (1992). A quality margin in transport. In: *Traffic Engineering and Control.* 33 (12). 661-665.

Gordon, P., Moore, J. E. I. and Richardson, H. W. (2002). *Economic-Engineering Integrated Models for Earthquakes: Socioeconomic Impacts.* 2002/19. PEER Report. Pacific Earthquake Engineering Research Center: College of Engineering, University of California, Berkeley.

Gordon, P., Richardson, H. W. and Davis, B. (1998). Transport-Related Impacts of the Northridge Earthquake. In: *Journal of Transportation and Statistics.* 1 (2). 21-36.

Green, C. and Van der Veen, A. (2007). *Indirect economic damage: concepts and guidelines.* Report. FLOODsite Project Deliverable D9.1, T09-06-01: Evaluating flood damages: guidance and recommendations on principles and methods. 16.02.2007. HR Wallingford, UK.

Grubesic, T. H. and Murray, A. T. (2006). Vital Nodes, Interconnected Infrastructures, and the Geographies of Network Survivability. In: *Annals of the Association of American Geographers.* 96 (1). 64-83.

Grünthal, G. (2004). Erdbeben und Erdbebengefährdung in Deutschland sowie im europäischen Kontext. In: *Geographie und Schule.* 151. 14-23.

Grünthal, G., Mayer-Rosa, D. and Lenhardt, W. A. (1998). Abschätzung der Erdbebengefährdung für die D-A-CH-Staaten - Deutschland, Österreich, Schweiz. In: *Bautechnik.* 10. 753-767.

Grünthal, G. and Wahlström, R. (2003). An Mw based earthquake catalogue for central, northern and northwestern Europe using a hierarchy of magnitude conversions. In: *Journal of Seismology.* 7. 507-531.

Grünthal, G. ed. (1998). *European Macroseismic Scale 1998 (EMS-98).* 15. Cahiers du Centre Européen de Géodynamique et de Séismologie. Centre Europèen de Géodynamique et de Séismologie: Luxembourg.

Guiliano, G. and Golob, J. (1998). Impacts of the Northridge Earthquake on Transit and Highway Use. In: *Journal of Transportation and Statistics.* 1 (2). 1-20.

Gunn, H. (2001). Spatial and temporal transferability of relationships between travel demand, trip cost and travel time. In: *Transportation Research Part E*. 37 (2-3). 163-189.

Gunn, H. F. (2008). An introduction to the valuation of travel-time savings and losses. In: *Handbook of transport modelling*. Hensher, D. A. and Button, K. J. (Eds.). Elsevier Science: Oxford. 503-517.

Haimes, Y. Y. and Jiang, P. (2001). Leontief-Based Model of Risk in Complex Interconnected Infrastructures. In: *Journal of Infrastructure Systems*. 7 (1). 1-12.

Ham, H., Kim, T. J. and Boyce, D. (2005a). Implementation and estimation of a combined model of interregional, multimodal commodity shipments and transportation network flows. In: *Transportation Research Part B*. 39. 65-79.

Ham, H., Kim, T. J. and Boyce, D. E. (2005b). Assessment of economic impacts from unexpected events with an interregional commodity flow and multimodal transportation network model. In: *Transportation Research Part A*. 39 (10). 849-860.

Hansen, M. and Sutter, J. (1990). *The Shake With Freight: The Impact of the Loma Prieta Earthquake On Bay Area Truckers*. Studies on the Loma Prieta Earthquake. The University of California Transportation Center: Berkeley, CA.

Heneka, P., Hofherr, T., Ruck, B. and Kottmeier, C. (2006). Winter storm risk of residential structures - model development and application to the German state of Baden-Württemberg. In: *Natural Hazards and Earth System Sciences*. 6. 721-733.

Hensher, D. A. and Figliozzi, M. A. (2007). Behavioural insight into the modelling of freight transportation and distribution systems. In: *Transportation Research Part B*. 41. 921-923.

Hilty, L. M., Page, B., Meyer, R., Mügge, H., Deecke, H. and Poll, M. (1996). *Konzeption eines Systems zur Abschätzung der Auswirkungen verkehrsbezogener Maßnahmen auf die Umwelt - MOBILE-Report Nr. 1*. FBI-HH-B-184/96. Report Series of the Department of Computer Science. University of Hamburg - Computer Science Department: Hamburg.

Hinsch, K., Krause, G. and Maerschalk, G. (2001). *Standardprognose des Erhaltungsbedarfs der Fernstraßeninfrastruktur bis 2015*. Report. Prepared for the Bundesministeriums für Verkehr, Bau- und Wohnungswesen. Project No. 28.004/1999/. ARGE SEP Maerschalk/RS-Consult Rübensam: Munich, Berlin.

Ho, P., Sussman, J. and Veneziano, D. (2001). *Estimating the direct and indirect losses from a midwest earthquake*. Report. Project SE-10: Economic Loss Estimation. Mid-America Earthquake Center: Urbana, IL.

Hogrebe, P., Platz, H. and Rieken, P. (1986). *Gesamtwirtschaftliche Bewertung von Verkehrswegeinvestitionen : Bewertungsverfahren für den Bundesverkehrswegeplan 1985*. Schriftenreihe des Bundesministers für Verkehr, 69. Bundesminister für Verkehr: Bonn-Bad Godesberg.

Holmgren, A. J. (2007). A Framework for Vulnerability Assessment of Electric Power Systems. In: *Critical Infrastructure - Reliability and Vulnerability*. Murray, A. T. and Grubesic, T. H. (Eds.). Springer: Berlin, Heidelberg. 31-55.

IKoNE (2006). *Aktionsplan Hochwasser Neckar - Update of 2002*. Brochure. Regierungspräsidium Stuttgart, Geschäftsstelle IKoNE: Stuttgart. http://www.ikone-online.de/fileadmin/user_upload/hw-ap_neckar/AP_Neckar_2002_-_2_01.pdf [9.3.2011].

infas and DIW (2003). *Mobilität in Deutschland: MiT 2002 - Mobilität in Tabellen*. Report. FE-Nr. 70.0736/2003. Bundesministerium für Verkehr, Bau und Stadtentwicklung: Berlin/Bonn.

Institut für Wasser und Gewässerentwicklung (2005). *Abgrenzung von Hochwassergefahrenflächen für die Städte Stuttgart und Esslingen*. Restricted research report. Universitaet Karlsruhe (TH), Institut für Wasser und Gewässerentwicklung, Bereich Wasserwirtschaft und Kulturtechnik, Prof. Dr.-Ing. F. Nestmann, for the Cities of Stuttgart and Esslingen: Karlsruhe.

Japan International Cooperation Agency (JICA) (2002). *The study on a disaster prevention/mitigation basic plan in Istanbul including seismic microzonation in the Republic of Turkey*. Final report. Istanbul Metropolitan Municipality (IMM)

Jenelius, E. (2007a). Geography and road network vulnerability: regional equity vs. economic efficiency. In: *Proceedings of the 9th Nectar Conference*. 9.-12.05.2007 in Porto, Portugal.

Jenelius, E. (2007b). Incorporating dynamics and information in a consequence model for road network vulnerability analysis. In: *Proceedings of the 3rd International Symposium on Transport Network Reliability (INSTR)*. 19.-20.07.2007 in The Hague, The Netherlands.

Jenelius, E. (2009). Network structure and travel patterns: explaining the geographical disparities of road network vulnerability. In: *Journal of Transport Geography*. 17. 234-244.

Jenelius, E. (2010). User inequity implications of road network vulnerability. In: *Journal of Transport and Land Use*. 2 (3/4). 57-73.

Jenelius, E., Petersen, T. and Mattsson, L.-G. (2006). Importance and exposure in road network vulnerability analysis. In: *Transportation Research Part A*. 40. 537-560.

Jenks, G. F. (1967). The data model concept in statistical mapping. In: *International yearbook of cartography*. 7. 186-190.

Jones, P. M. (1979). New approaches to understanding travel behaviour: The human activity approach. In: *Behavioural travel modelling*. Hensher, D. A. and Stopher, P. R. (Eds.). Croom Helm: London. 55-80.

Karlsruhe Cluster for Disaster Research (2006). *Draft Proposal for the Establishment and Funding of the Cluster of Excellence*. Restricted draft proposal submitted to the DFG. 01.09.2006.

Khazai, B., Merz, M., Schulz, C. and Borst, D. (2011). An Integrated Indicator Framework for Spatial Assessment of Industrial and Social Vulnerability to Indirect Disaster Losses. In: *Natural Hazards*. Submitted 26.01.2011. In review process.

Kim, E., Hewings, G. J. D. and Hong, C. (2004). An Application of an Integrated Transport Network–Multiregional CGE Model: a Framework for the Economic Analysis of Highway Projects. In: *Economic Systems Research*. 16 (3). 235-258.

Kim, T. J., Ham, H. and Boyce, D. E. (2002). Economic impacts of transportation network changes: Implementation of a combined transportation network and input-output model. In: *Papers in Regional Science*. 81. 223-246.

Kleist, L., Thieken, A. H., Köhler, P., Müller, M., Seifert, I., Borst, D. and Werner, U. (2006). Estimation of the regional stock of residential buildings as a basis for a comparative risk assessment in Germany. In: *Natural Hazards and Earth System Sciences*. 6. 541-552.

Kunert, U. (2010). Abschätzung von Schäden im Verkehrssektor. In: *Hochwasserschäden - Erfassung, Abschätzung und Vermeidung*. Thieken, A. H., Seifert, I. and Merz, B. (Eds.). Oekom: München. 235-252.

Landesbetrieb Straßenbau Nordrhein-Westfalen (2006). *NRW-Offensive gegen den Verkehrsstau. Konzepte und Maßnahmen für die Zukunft.* Brochure. Straßen.NRW: Gelsenkirchen.

Latora, V. and Marchiori, M. (2004). How the science of complex networks can help developing strategies against terrorism. In: *Chaos, Solitons and Fractals*. 20. 69-75.

Leitstelle Wiederaufbau (2003). *Augusthochwasser 2003 - Schadensausgleich und Wiederaufbau im Freistaat Sachsen*. Brochure. Staatskanzlei Freistaat Sachsen: Dresden.

Lenz, S. (2009). *Vulnerabilität kritischer Infrastrukturen*. Forschung im Bevölkerungsschutz. Bundesamt für Bevölkerungsschutz und Katastrophenhilfe: Bonn.

Liedtke, G. (2006). *An actor-based approach to commodity transport modelling*. Nomos: Baden-Baden.

Little, R. G. (2002). Controlling Cascading Failure: Understanding the Vulnerabilities of Interconnected Infrastructures. In: *Journal of Urban Technology*. 9 (1). 109-123.

Lohse, D. (2004). *Travel demand modelling with model EVA - Simultaneous model for trip generation, trip distribution and mode choice. Summary report.* Brochure. http://vplno1.vkw.tu-dresden.de/vpl/viseva/Download/Viseva-engl.pdf [9.3.2011].

Lohse, D., Bachner, G., Dugge, B. and Teichert, H. (1997). *Ermittlung von Verkehrsströmen mit n-linearen Gleichungssystemen unter Beachtung von Nebenbedingungen einschließlich Parameterschätzung (Verkehrsnachfragemodellierung: Erzeugung, Verteilung, Aufteilung)*. Schriftenreihe des Instituts für Verkehrsplanung und Straßenverkehr. Institut für Verkehrsplanung und Straßenverkehr: Dresden.

Lüders, S. and Schulz, C. (2010). Auswirkung von Naturkatastrophen auf das Verkehrsverhalten. In: *Working Documents of Freight Transport and Logistics*. 4. urn:nbn:de:swb:90-200580.

Mackie, P. J., Fowkes, A. S., Wardman, M., Whelan, G., Nellthorp, J. and Bates, J. (2003). *Value of travel time savings in the UK: summary report*. Summary report. Department for Transport: London.

Maibach, M., Schreyer, C., Sutter, D., van Essen, H. P., Boon, B. H., Smokers, R., Schroten, A., Doll, C., Pawlowska, B. and Bak, M. (2008). *Handbook on estimation of external costs in the transport sector - Internalisation measures and policies for all external cost of transport (IMPACT)*. Version 1.1. CE Delft: Delft.

Manski, C. F. (1973). *The analysis of qualitative choice*. Dissertation. Massachusetts Institute of Technology.

Markau, H.-J. (2003). *Risikobetrachtung von Naturgefahren: Analyse, Bewertung und Management des Risikos von Naturgefahren am Beispiel der sturmflutgefährdeten Küstenniederungen Schleswig-Holsteins*. Dissertation. Christian-Albrecht-Universität zu Kiel.

McFadden, D. (1974). Conditional logit analysis of qualitative choice behavior. In: *Frontiers in econometrics*. Zarembka, P. (Eds.). Academic Press: London. 105-142.

Mechler, R. (2004). *Natural Disaster Risk Management and Financing Disaster Losses in Developing Countries*. Verlag für Versicherungswirtschaft: Karlsruhe.

Meskouris, K., Renault, P., Butenweg, C., Hinzen, K. G. and Weber, B. (2007). *Gefährdungsabschätzung von Brücken in Deutschland unter Erdbebenbelastung*. Forschung Straßenbau und Straßenverkehrstechnik, 952. Bundesministerium für Verkehr, Bau und Stadtentwicklung: Berlin.

Meyer, V. and Messner, F. (2005). National flood damage evaluation methods - a review of applied methods in England, the Netherlands, the Czech Republic and Germany. In: *UFZ Discussion Papers*. 21/2005.

Morris, J. M., Dumble, P. L. and Wigan, M. R. (1979). Accessibility indicators for transportation planning. In: *Transportation Research Part A*. 13. 91-109.

Much, H. (22.6.2010). *Brückensanierung mit Staugefahr - Ab heute ist die B 463 für fünf Monate halbseitig gesperrt – Umleitung für Pkws in Richtung Balingen*. Zollern Alb Kurier. 22.6.2010. http://www.zak.de/artikel/90044/Albstadt-Ebingen-Brueckensanierung-mit-Staugefahr [17.12.2010].

Münchener Rückversicherungs-Gesellschaft (2011a). *Great natural catastrophes worldwide 1950 - 2010 - Percentage distribution per event group*. Geo Risk Research, NatCatSERVICE. [8.9.2011a].

Münchener Rückversicherungs-Gesellschaft (2011b). *Great weather catastrophes worldwide 1950 - 2010 - Number of events with trend.* Geo Risk Research, NatCatSERVICE. [8.9.2011b].

Münchner Rückversicherungs-Gesellschaft (1999). *Naturkatastrophen in Deutschland: Schadenerfahrungen und Schadenpotentiale*. Brochure. Münchner Rückversicherungs-Gesellschaft: München.

Münchner Rückversicherungs-Gesellschaft (2003). *Risk-Management Tunnel*. Brochure. Münchner Rückversicherungs-Gesellschaft: München.

Nagurney, A. and Qiang, Q. (2007a). A network efficiency measure for congested networks. In: *Europhysics Letters*. 79 (3/38005).

Nagurney, A. and Qiang, Q. (2007b). A Transportation Network Efficiency Measure that Captures Flows, Behaviours, and Costs with Applications to Network Component Importance Identification and Vulnerability. In: *Proceedings of the POMS 18th Annual Conference*. 04.-05.05.2007 in Dallas, Texas, USA. 1-22.

Nagurney, A. and Qiang, Q. (2007c). Robustness of transportation networks subject to degradable links. In: *Europhysics Letters*. 80 (6/68001).

Nagurney, A. and Qiang, Q. (2008). A network efficiency measure with application to critical infrastructure networks. In: *Journal of Global Optimisation*. 40. 261-275.

Nagurney, A. and Qiang, Q. (2009). A Relative Total Cost Index for the Evaluation of Transportation Network Robustness in the Presence of Degradable Links and Alternative Travel Behaviour. In: *International Transactions in Operational Research*. 16 (1). 49-67.

Nagurney, A., Qiang, Q. and Nagurney, L. S. (2010). Environmental impact assessment of transportation networks with degradable links in an era of climate change. In: *International Journal of Sustainable Transportation*. 4 (3). 154-171.

Nardo, M., Saisana, M., Saltelli, M., Tarantola, S., Hoffman, A. and Giovannini, E. (2005). *Handbook on constructing composite indicators: methodology and user guide*. OECD Statistics Working Papers. 2005/3. OECD Publishing: Paris. doi:10.1787/533411815016.

National Transportation Safety Board (2008). *Highway Accident Report: Collapse of I-35W Highway Bridge Minneapolis, Minnesota August 1, 2007*. Report. NTSB/HAR-08/03, PB2008-916203, Notation 7975C. National Transportation Safety Board: Washington D.C.

NEA, IWW, COWI, NESTEAR, PWC Italy, TINA, IVT, HERRY and MKmetric (2004). *Final report of the TEN-STAC project funded by the European Commission (DG TREN)*. Final report.

Odgaard, T., Kelly, C. and Laird, J. (2005). *HEATCO Work Package 3: Current practice in project appraisal in Europe*. Report. Deliverable 1, Volume 1. European Commission EC-DG TREN: Brussels.

Okuyama, Y. (2007). Economic Modeling for Disaster Impact Analysis: Past, Present, and Future. In: *Economic System Research*. 19 (2). 115-124.

Okuyama, Y. (2009). *Critical review of methodologies on disaster impact estimation.* Background Paper for Assessment on the Economics of Disaster Risk reduction. Global Facility for Disaster Research and Recovery (GFDRR), Worldbank: Washington.

Oppenheim, N. (1995). *Urban travel demand modeling - From individual choices to general equilibrium.* John Wiley & Sons: New York, NY.

Ortuzar, J. d. D. (1982). Fundamentals of discrete multimodal choice modelling. In: *Transport Reviews.* 2 (1). 47-78.

Ortuzar, J. d. D. and Willumsen, L. G. (2004). *Modelling Transport.* Wiley: Chichester.

Ott, A. (2006). *Privatwirtschaftliche Infrastrukturkosten eines Eisenbahnunternehmens.* Karlsruher Beiträge zur wirtschaftspolitischen Forschung, 21. Rothengatter, W. and Kowalski, J. (Eds.). Nomos: Baden-Baden.

Ott, A. and Schulz, C. (2007). Risk assessment of railway infrastructure networks due to force majeure. In: *Proeceedings of the EURNEX-Žel: Towards more competitive European rail system.* 30.-31.05.2007 in Žilina, Slovakia. Volume 2. 220-227.

PCC RARM (1997). *Framework for the environmental health risk management.* Final Report Vol. 1. The Presidential/Congressional Commission on Risk Assessment and Risk Management (PCC RARM): Washington DC.

Pederson, P., Dudenhoeffer, D., Hartley, S. and Permann, M. (2006). *Critical Infrastructure Interdependency Modeling: A Survey of U.S. and International Research.* Report. INL/EXT-06-11464, August 2006. Idaho National Laboratory: Idaho Falls, Idaho.

Peters, K., Buzna, L. and Helbing, D. (2008). Modelling of cascading effects and efficient response to disaster spreading in complex networks. In: *International Journal of Critical Infrastructures.* 4 (1/2). 46-62.

Planco Consulting GmbH (2000). *Numerische Aktualisierung interner und externer Beförderungskosten für die Bundesverkehrswegeplanung (BVWP) auf den Preisstand des Jahres 1998.* Final Report, November 2000, FE-Nr. 96.602/1999. Planco Consulting GmbH for the Bundesministerium für Verkehr, Bau- und Wohnungswesen.

Platz, U. (2005). *Vulnerabilität von Logistikstrukturen im Lebensmittelhandel. Eine Studie zu den Logistikstrukturen des Lebensmittelhandels, möglichen Gefahrenquellen und den Auswirkungen verschiedener Gefahren bei einem Ereigniseintritt.* Schriftenreihe des Bundesministeriums für Ernährung, Landwirtschaft und Verbraucherschutz. Reihe A: Angewandte Wissenschaft, Heft 512. Landwirtschaftsverlag: Münster-Hiltrup.

Platz, U. (2007). Vulnerability of logistic structures in food trade. In: *Proceedings of the 8th Forum DKKV/CEDIM: Disaster Reduction in Climate Change.* 15.-16.10.2007 in Karlsruhe, Germany.

PTV AG (2009). *Visum 11.0 Grundlagen.* PTV AG: Karlsruhe.

Reed, D. A., Chang, S. E., McDaniels, T. and Longstaf, H. (2007). Modeling Interdependent Lifeline System Behavior for Hurricane Scenarios. In: *Proceedings of the Twelfth In-*

ternational Conference on Wind Engineering (ICWE12). 01.-06.07.2007 in Cairns, Australia.

Rinaldi, S. M., Peerenboom, J. P. and Kelly, T. K. (2001). Critical Infrastructure Interdependencies. In: *IEEE Control Systems Magazine*. 21 (6). 11-25.

Rommerskirchen, S., Rothengatter, W., Greinus, A., Leypoldt, P., Liedtke, G. and Scholz, A. (2009). *Life cycle cost analysis of infrastructure networks - the case of the German federal trunk roads*. Karlsruhe Papers in Economic Policy Research, 27. Nomos: Baden-Baden.

Sächsisches Landesamt für Umwelt und Geologie (2004). *Ereignisanalyse -Hochwasser August 2002 in den Osterzgebirgsflüssen. Managementreport*. Report. LII-1/27. Sächsisches Landesamt für Umwelt und Geologie, Freistaat Sachsen: Dresden.

Sakakibara, H., Kajitani, Y. and Okada, N. (2004). Road network robustness for avoiding functional isolation in disasters. In: *Journal of Transportation Engineering*. 130 (5). 560-567.

Schoch, M. (2004). *Verwendung feinräumiger geographischer Informationen in aggregierten Verkehrsprognosen*. Karlsruhe Papers in Economic Policy Research, 15. Rothengatter, W. and Kowalski, J. (Eds.). Nomos: Baden-Baden.

Schulz, C. (2007). Identification of critical transport infrastructures. In: *Proceedings of the 8.Forum DKKV/CEDIM: Disaster Reduction in Climate Change*. 15.-16.10.2007 in Karlsruhe, Germany.

Schweizerische Eidgenossenschaft (2009). *Grundstrategie des Bundesrates zum Schutz Kritischer Infratrukturen - Basis für die nationale Strategie zum Schutz Kritischer Infratrukturen*. Brochure. Schweizerische Eidgenossenschaft - der Bundesrat. http://www.bevoelkerungsschutz.admin.ch/internet/bs/de/home/themen/ski/publikationen_ski.parsys.60516.downloadList.62742.DownloadFile.tmp/grundstrategieski20090518d.pdf [17.8.2010].

Seifert, I., Thieken, A. H., Merz, M., Borst, D. and Werner, U. (2010). Estimation of industrial and commercial asset values for hazard risk assessment. In: *Natural Hazards*. 52. 453-479.

Setola, R., De Procellinis, S. and Sforna, M. (2009). Critical infrastrcuture dependency assessment using the input-output inoperability model. In: *International Journal of Critical Infrastructure Protection*. 2. 170-178.

Shinozuka, M. and Chang, S. E. (2004). Evaluating Disaster Resilience of Power Networks and Grids. In: *Modeling spatial and economic impact of disasters*. Okuyama, Y. and Chang, S. E. (Eds.). Springer: Berlin and Heidelberg.

Shinozuka, M., Grigoriu, M., Ingraffea, A. R., Billington, S. L., Feenstra, P., Soong, T. T., Reinhorn, A. M. and Maragakis, E. (2000). Development of Fragility Imformation for Structures and Nonstructural Components. In: *Research Progress and Accomplishments*. 1999-2000. 15-32.

Sohn, J., Hewings, G. J. D., Kim, T. J., Lee, J. S. and Jang, S.-G. (2004). Analysis of Economic Impacts of an earthquake on Transportation Network. In: *Modeling spatial and economic impact of disasters*. Okuyama, Y. a. C. S. E. (Eds.). Springer: Berlin and Heidelberg.

Sohn, J., Kim, T. J., Hewings, G. J. D., Lee, J. S. and Jang, S.-G. (2003). Retrofit Priority of Transport Network Links under an Earthquake. In: *Journal of Urban Planning and Development*. 129 (4). 195-210.

Spiegel Online GmbH (9.8.2007). *Hochwasser in Süddeutschland - Rhein-Anwohner rüsten sich für die Flut*. SPIEGEL ONLINE. 9.8.2007. http://www.spiegel.de/panorama/0,1518,499173,00.html [17.8.2010].

SSP Consult (2003). *Verbesserung des Verkehrsablaufs auf Fernstraßen in Baden-Württemberg - Störfallanalyse und Maßnahmenkonzept*. Final report (restricted). Ministerium für Umwelt und Verkehr Baden-Wuerttemberg represented by Landesstelle für Straßentechnik. SSP Consult Beratende Ingenieure GmbH: Stuttgart.

Statistische Ämter des Bundes und der Länder (2011). *Volkswirtschaftliche Gesamtrechnungen der Länder: Bruttoinlandsprodukt – in jeweiligen Preisen – 1991 bis 2010*. Status: August 2010/ February 2011. Statistisches Landesamt Baden-Württemberg (Ed.): Stuttgart. http://www.vgrdl.de/Arbeitskreis_VGR/tbls/tab01.asp [08.07.2011].

Statistische Landesämter (2007). *Statistik lokal - Daten für die Gemeinden, kreisfreien Städte und Kreise Deutschlands*. Status 31.12.2005, CD-Rom. Statistische Landesämter des Bundes und der Länder.

Statistisches Landesamt Baden-Württemberg (2010). *Jahresfahrleistungen im Straßenverkehr in Baden-Württemberg seit 1980 nach Straßenkategorien und Fahrzeugarten*. Status: February 2010. Statistisches Landesamt Baden-Württemberg: Stuttgart. http://www.statistik.baden-wuerttemberg.de/ [24.03.2010].

Straßenbauverwaltung Baden-Württemberg (2007). *Verkehrsstärken 2005*. Map. Straßenbauverwaltung Baden-Württemberg.

SWR Politik und Gesellschaft (1999). *Der Orkan Lothar und seine Folgen*. Radio feature in SWR1 - Thema heute, 27.12.1999, 19:30h - 20:00h. Archive No.:W010936. Baden-Baden.

SWR1 Aktuell (1999). *Orkan Lothar fällt reihenweise Bäume*. Radio feature in SWR1 Aktuell, 26.12.1999, 12:00h - 13:00h. Archive No.:W131183. Baden-Baden.

SWR1 Aktuelle Information (2007). *Sturm Kyrill*. Radio feature in SWR1 Tagesthema, 18.1.2007, 17:05h - 18:00h. Archive No.:W138352. Baden-Baden.

Szimba, E. (2008). *Interdependence between transport infrastructure projects - an analytical framework applied to priority transport infrastructure projects of the European Union*. Karlsruhe Papers in Economic Policy Research, 25. Rothengatter, W. and Kowalski, J. (Eds.). Nomos: Baden-Baden.

Taubenböck, H., Post, J., Roth, A., Zosseder, K., Strunz, G. and Dech, S. (2008). A conceptual vulnerability and risk framework as outline to identify capabilities of remote sensing. In: *Natural Hazards and Earth System Sciences*. 8 (3). 409-420.

Taylor, M. A. P. and D'Este, G. M. (2004). Critical infrastructure and transport network vulnerability: developing a method for diagnosis and assessment. In: *Proceedings of the Second International Symposium on Transportation Network Reliability*. 20.-24.08.2004 in Christchurch and Queenstown, New Zealand. 96-102.

Taylor, M. A. P. and D'Este, G. M. (2007). Transport Network Vulnerability: a Method for Diagnosis of Critical Locations in Transport Infrastructure Systems. In: *Critical Infrastructure - Reliability and Vulnerability*. Murray, A. T. and Grubesic, T. H. (Eds.). Springer: Berlin, Heidelberg. 9-30.

Taylor, M. A. P., Sekhar, S. V. C. and D'Este, G. M. (2006). Application of Accessibility Base Methods for Vulnerability Analysis of Strategic Road Networks. In: *Networks and Spatial Economics*. 6. 267-291.

Thieken, A. H., Müller, M., Kleist, L., Seifert, I., Borst, D. and Werner, U. (2006). Regionalisation of asset values for risk analysis. In: *Natural Hazards and Earth System Sciences*. 6. 167-178.

Thywissen, K. (2006). *Components of Risk: A Comparative Glossary*. SOURCE. UNU Institute for Environment and Human Security (UNU-EHS): Bonn, Germany.

Tierney, K. J. (1995). Impacts of Recent Disasters on Businesses: The 1993 Midwest Floods and the 1994 Northridge Earthquake. In: *Proceedings of the National Center for Earthquake Engineering Research Conference on the Economic Impacts of Catastrophic Earthquakes - Anticipating the Unexpected*. 12.-13.09.1995 in New York, USA.

Tierney, K. J. (1997). Business Impacts of the Northridge Earthquake. In: *Journal of Contingencies and Crisis Management*. 5 (2). 87-97.

Tilahun, N. and Levinson, D. (2008). *I-35W Bridge collapse: travel impacts and adjustment strategies*. CiteSeerX Working Paper. http://nexus.umn.edu/Papers/I-35wTravelImpactsandAdjustmentStrategies.pdf [19.8.2010].

TINA, Dorsch Consult, IWW, NEA, NESTEAR, Su-Yapi and Geomatic (2007). *Technical Assistance to Transport Infrastructure Needs Assessment on behalf of the European Commission and CFCU (Central Finance and Contracts Unit), Ankara*. Final report.

Train, K. E. (2003). *Discrete choice methods with simulation*. Cambridge University Press: New York, NY.

TRT and CSIL (2008). *Guide to cost-benefit analysis of investment projects: structural Funds, cohesion fund and instrument for pre-accession*. Final report. Prepared by Trasporti e Territorio (TRT) and Centre for Industrial Studies (CSIL). 16/06/2008. European Commission - Directorate General Regional Policy: Brussels.

Tukey, J. W. (1977). *Exploratory data analysis*. Addison-Wesley series in behavioral science: quantitative methods. Addison-Wesley: Reading, Massachusetts.

Tyagunov, S., Grünthal, G., Wahlström, R., Stempniewski, L. and Zschau, J. (2006a). Earthquake Damage and Loss Estimation on a Regional Scale. In: *Proceedings of the First European Conference on Earthquake Engineering and Seismology*. 03.-08.09.2006 in Geneva, Switzerland. Paper No. 311.

Tyagunov, S., Grünthal, G., Wahlström, R., Stempniewski, L. and Zschau, J. (2006b). Seismic risk mapping for Germany. In: *Natural Hazards and Earth System Sciences*. 6. 573-586.

Tyagunov, S., Schulz, C., Wenzel, F., Stempniewski, L. and Kostenko, M. (2007). Modelling and analysis of transportation networks in earthquake prone areas. In: *Proceedings of the 18th Pacific Conference on Earthquake Engineering (8PCEE) 2007*. 05.-07.12.2007 in Singapore. Paper No. 210.

UCTE (2007). *Final Report: System Disturbance on 4 November 2006*. Final report. Union for the Coordination of Transmission of Electricity (UCTE): Brussels, Belgium.

UVM (17.3.2010). *Tanja Gönner dankt Räum- und Streudiensten für unermüdliches Engagement*. Press release. 17.3.2010. Ministerium für Umwelt, Naturschutz und Verkehr (UVM): Stuttgart. http://www.baden-wuerttemberg.de/de/Tanja_Goenner_dankt_Raeum-_und_Streudiensten_fuer_unermuedliches_Engagement/227639.html?referer=88434 [9.3.2011].

van de Kaa, E. J. (2010). Sign-dependent value of time in stated preference: Judgement bias or exposure of genuine preference? In: *European Journal of Transport and Infrastructure Research*. 10 (4). 347-367.

Van der Veen, A. (2003). In search of a common methodology on damage estimation: from the economist's perspective. In: *In search of a common methodology on damage estimation. Workshop Proceedings*. Van der Veen, A., Vetere Arellano, A. L. and Nordvik, J.-P. (Eds.). European Communities: 4-10.

Van der Veen, A. and Logtmeijer, C. (2005). Economic Hotspots: Visualizing Vulnerability to Flooding. In: *Natural Hazards*. 36. 65-80.

Waha, E. (2009). *Die Autobahn ist schneller schwarz*. Nordbayerischer Kurier. 16.7.2009. 2009. http://www.nordbayerischer-kurier.de/nachrichten/1282626/details_8.htm [9.3.2011].

Wardman, M. (1998). The value of travel time: A review of British evidence. In: *Journal of Transport Economics and Policy*. 32 (3). 285-316.

Wardrop, J. G. (1952). Some theoretical aspects of road traffic research. In: *ICE Proceedings: Engineering Divisions*. 1 (3). 325-362.

Wermuth, M. (2005). Modellvorstellungen zur Prognose. In: *Stadtverkehrsplanung - Grundlagen, Methoden, Ziele*. Steierwald, G., Künne, H. D. and Vogt, W. (Eds.). Springer: Berlin/Heidelberg. 243-295.

Wezel, H. U., Bauer-Hailer, U., Einwiller, R., Knödler, R. and Fischer, B. (2010). *Baden-Württemberg - ein Standort im Vergleich.* Brochure. Statistisches Landesamt Baden-Württemberg: Stuttgart.

Willeke, R. and Paulußen, U. (1991). *Berücksichtigung projektbedingter Ersparnisse an Reisezeit im nicht-gewerblichen Personenverkehr bei der Planung von Verkehrswegen des Bundes.* Final Report, FE-Nr: 90227/90. Institut für Verkehrswissenschaft at Universität zu Köln for the Minister of Transport.

Willson, R. (1998). Impacts and Responses: Goods Movement After the Northridge Earthquake. In: *Journal of Transportation and Statistics.* 1 (2). 37-48.

Wirtschaftsministerium Baden-Württemberg (2010). *Das überörtliche Verkehrsnetz Baden-Württemberg.* http://www.logistik-bw.de/Road.57+M54a708de802.0.html. [20.7.2010].

Wisetjindawat, W., Sano, K., Matsumoto, S. and Raothanachonkun, P. (2007). Micro-simulation model for modeling freight agents interactions in urban freight movement. In: *Proceedings of the 86th Annual Meeting of the Transportation Research Board.* 21.-25.01.2007 in Washington D.C., USA. Paper Number 07-2224.

Yamano, N., Kajitani, Y. and Shumuta, Y. (2007). Modeling the Regional Economic Loss of Natural Disasters: The Search for Economic Hotspots. In: *Economic System Research.* 19 (2). 163-181.

Yamazaki, F. (2001). Applications of remote sensing and GIS for damage assessment. In: *Structural Safety and Reliability: Proceedings of the Eighth International Conference, ICOSSAR '01.* Corotis, R. B., Shinozuka, M. and Schuëller, G. I. (Eds.). Swets & Zeitlinger: Lisse, The Netherlands. 1-12.

Yao, E. and Morikawa, T. (2005). A study of an integrated intercity travel demand model. In: *Transportation Research Part A.* 39. 367-381.

Zhang, P. and Peeta, S. (2011). A generalized modeling framework to analyze interdependencies among infrastructure systems. In: *Transportation Research Part B.* 45 (3). 553-579.

Zhang, W. J., Liu, X., Chai, C.-L., Deters, R., Liu, D., Dyachuk, D., Tu, Y. L. and Baber, Z. (2008). Social network analysis of the vulnerabilities of interdependent critical infrastructures. In: *International Journal of Critical Infrastructures.* 4 (3). 256-273.

Zhu, S. and Levinson, D. (2009). *A review of research on planned and unplanned disruptions to transportation networks.* CiteSeerX Working Paper. http://nexus.umn.edu/Papers/DisruptionReview.pdf [19.8.2010].

Zhu, S., Levinson, D., Liu, H. and Harder, K. (2010). The traffic and behavioral effects of the I-35W Mississippi River bridge collapse. In: *Proceedings of the TRB 88th Annual Meeting 2009.* 11.-15.01.2009 in Washington, D.C., USA.